LOST DOGS MUST TRAVEL

BEST OF MISSOURI
A Guide to Dog-Friendly Hotels, Hikes, Restaurants, and More

JUSTINE RIGGS

REEDY PRESS
St. Louis, Missouri

Copyright © 2013 by Justine Riggs

Reedy Press
PO Box 5131
St. Louis, MO 63139, USA

No part of this publication may be reproduced or transmitted in any form or by any means, electronic or mechanical, including photocopy, recording, or any information storage and retrieval system, without permission in writing from the publisher.

Permissions may be sought directly from Reedy Press at the above mailing address or via our website at www.reedypress.com.

Library of Congress Control Number: 2013935558

ISBN: 978-1-935806-45-5

Please visit our website at www.reedypress.com.

Design by Jill Halpin

Printed in the United States of America
13 14 15 16 17   5 4 3 2 1

CONTENTS

Introduction	v
Kansas City Region	**1**
Northwest Region	**14**
Chillicothe	14
Northeast Region	**21**
Hannibal	21
Kirksville	28
Central Region	**35**
Columbia	35
Fulton	47
Hermann	57
Jefferson City	67
Lake of the Ozarks	77
St. Louis Region	**87**
St. Charles County	87
St. Louis	101
Whine Trail	122
Southwest Region	**127**
Branson	127
Carthage	139
Springfield	147
Southeast Region	**163**
Arcadia Valley	163
Cape Girardeau	173
Indexes	**185**

Missouri

- Kirksville
- Chillicothe
- Hannibal
- Kansas City
- Columbia
- Fulton
- St. Charles
- Hermann
- Whine Trail
- St. Louis
- Jefferson City
- Lake of the Ozarks
- Arcadia Valley
- Cape Girardeau
- Carthage
- Springfield
- Branson

INTRODUCTION

Dogs make great traveling partners. They look adorable riding shotgun, they never ask if we're there yet, and you don't have to play the alphabet game with them. An occasional pat on the head and small talk suits them just fine.

Fortunately for travelers, the Show Me State caters to man's best friend. *Love Dogs, Must Travel* will guide you to Missouri's most dog-friendly accommodations, restaurants, activities, sites, shopping, and much more. *LDMT* is not meant to be an exhaustive resource to *everything* dog-friendly in Missouri. Instead, it's the pick of the litter, so to speak. For instance, the Springfield and Central areas of the state—along with the St. Louis and Kansas City regions—are extremely welcoming to dogs. Listings have been included for their friendliness toward dogs, pricing, special touches just for Fido, or for the ease of which you and your dog can participate together. Other entries made the cut due to unique or extra special qualities they possess.

While *LDMT* offers an abundance of travel options, you may stumble on additional activities or establishments along the way. Often, the highlight of the trip is something unforeseen or unplanned, so it's wise to schedule extra drive time. Besides, your pup will tell you that there's no such thing as too many potty breaks, and he'll want to stop to sniff around and stretch often.

Furthermore, you'll notice that some cities are not mentioned at all. Unfortunately, some towns that abound in human activity may not offer much to our furry companions. *LDMT* focuses on the destinations that offer our four-legged friends more than enough to keep their tails wagging and make visiting worth the drive for all.

Sister Weimaraners, Harlie and Kaia, are family in our household. They love going everywhere with me (not just the places where they get treats), and I miss them terribly when I have to leave them behind. Planning our first holiday trip together proved to be a challenge. Information about traveling with dogs was very limited, and much of the information I found was out of date. Thus, most entries that follow have a long, consistent track record for accommodating our furry friends.

Missouri is naturally beautiful, rich in history, and offers unique festivals and activities that allow you to include your pup. It has become increasingly common for travelers to take their dogs along with them, and more places are offering canine accommodations. Harlie, Kaia, and I wanted to eliminate the work for you, so we set out to find the best canine opportunities in the Show Me State and are excited to share them with you in *LDMT*.

FIDO FLEXIBILITY & PREPARED POOCHES

Vacations don't always go according to plan. Being prepared and flexible can save a failing trip! *LDMT* offers numerous options for a variety of towns and regions in Missouri, but it's always best to know where you're going and what to expect. Policies and events change, and websites are often dated. Calling ahead to confirm that your dog is welcome eliminates uncertainty and extra drive time. Plan B can always be found in the following pages!

Packing is an important part of traveling with your dog. You hope that medical attention is not part of your trip, but you'll be better prepared if you have what you need. Always carry your vet's information and a copy of your dog's **current vaccinations.** Also, know where emergency treatment is available in the area you are visiting.

Canine First Aid Kits are reasonably priced and can be purchased at many local stores, or you can easily assemble your own. Lists of items to include can be found online on numerous websites. A good one to start with is www.redcross.org. You may want to include other items based on recommendations from your vet and to suit your pup's individual needs. Make sure your kit includes a great pair of tweezers. They will undoubtedly come in handy when checking her paws or pulling off ticks after hikes (be timely with flea and tick prevention). Other helpful items include, but are not limited to, towels, paper towels, puppy-approved wipes, disinfectant wipes, and both small and large waste bags. Your dog will be most comfortable if you pack his favorite toys, pet bed, and blankets, along with travel bowls and anything else that suits his needs. In the case of inclement weather or that you are having so much fun that you decide to extend travel, you'll want to have extra medications and dog food on hand. Give some consideration to what you'll be doing on your trip and pack accordingly, tailoring your supplies to your specific needs. For example, if you plan on hiking on rough terrain and your pup's paws aren't conditioned for that, she'll need booties for protection.

EXTRA KIBBLES & BITS

I know it sounds completely absurd and is almost impossible to believe, but not all humans are dog lovers! Following puppy etiquette and being respectful allows us to get along and share space with others. It should go without saying, yet somehow it doesn't. **Pick up your dog's poo!** Respect others' property and find a place to stay that fits both of your needs. Look for accommodations—like those listed in the following pages—that have fenced yards or are close to parks or trails. In the event your dog makes a mess beyond simple cleanup or does damage, be up front and offer to compensate the owner of the property. In addition, avoid outdoor areas where pups are not allowed in order to avoid damage to natural habitats. Following these simple rules lessens the possibility of fee increases and canine bans.

Accommodating your dog will result in better behavior. Exercise your pooch before you head out for activities or long car rides. He'll be calmer and happier, which means you will be too. Attempt to follow his normal feeding and walking routine as best as you can and always carry a travel bowl and plenty of water. Let her drink often to avoid dehydration and stomach rolling in larger dogs. Treats come in handy as a reward or distraction. Do not put your dog in a social situation that makes her uncomfortable. Places that are too crowded or too noisy can result in a nervous dog with unexpected and undesirable behavior.

Temperature rises quickly in cars in warmer months, and just a few minutes can be devastating for your dog. In addition, many rest stops do not allow dogs to go inside the restroom with you. Travel with a partner so that the air conditioner and car can remain running. For current information about Missouri rest stops, including those with designated pet areas, visit www.modot.org/services.

Keep Fido leashed, as new smells and sights can distract and lure him away when in unfamiliar territory. He should be chipped, have current tags, and you should carry a picture ID of him in the unfortunate event that he gets lost. Always carry a leash when in off-leash areas in case you encounter problems with another dog or people who are afraid of dogs. It is also polite to move aside on paths and sidewalks to give pup-free pedestrians the right-of-way.

Finally, our pups just want to be with us. Humans often tend to put all the focus on the destination, but we shouldn't overlook the journey as a truly enjoyable part of traveling. Beauty abounds along the roads of the Show Me State, and the drive itself makes for great bonding time for you and Fido! *Love Dogs, Must Travel* pinpoints Missouri's top dog destinations in addition to treats along the way. By being flexible, preparing before you go, and following a few simple rules of courtesy, your road trip will be a huge success and you'll hardly be able to wait until the next time you hit the road together!

KANSAS CITY REGION

KANSAS CITY

Uniquely divided into districts such as Country Club Plaza, Westport, Crown Center, and the Crossroads Arts District, Kansas City is canine-friendly and a place where you and your pup will never run out of activities. One of the most popular areas within K.C. is Country Club Plaza. It's commonplace to find water bowls on the sidewalks for pups, furry friends dining with their companions on the patios of interesting eateries, as well as upscale shops that allow dogs to browse with their owners. A favorite time of year to visit is between Thanksgiving and Christmas when the entire Plaza is aglow with lights, causing even the scroogiest to get into the spirit of the season. Art is prominent on the streets of the Plaza, in the parks, and in other areas of the city. Numerous restaurants welcome your loyal companion to dine with you on their patios, and many of the hotels around town accommodate pups. In addition, there's no shortage of shops specializing in dog-friendly gear and products.

PARKS & TRAILS FOR TAILS

JACOB L. LOOSE PARK

No matter the time of year, beauty abounds at Loose Park. Near the Plaza at 5100 Wornall Road, this park is known for its rose gardens (approximately 4,000 roses in 150 different varieties), historical markers, and walkways skirting Loose Lake, among other interesting characteristics. It is one of the primary sites of the Battle of Westport, and it is the place where Major General Sterling Price was defeated by Union soldiers, forcing his troops to retreat to Arkansas. Visitors will find both the Battle of Westport Monument (six tons of red granite) and the Monnett Battle Field Cannon in the park. The Laura Conyers Smith Fountain, the Adam and Eve Fountain, trails, picnic and shelter areas, and even a rain garden are some of the other features of Loose Park. Go to www.kcmo.org to read about the Wrapped Walk Ways exhibit of 1978 and other unique areas at Loose Park.

PENN VALLEY PARK

This off-leash dog park has been open since 2004 and is just under three acres, with an additional area for dogs forty pounds and under. The park is open every day of the week from dawn to an hour after dusk and is free to visitors. It has seating, double-gated entries, and a water source. You and your pup can find this park at 29th and Wyandotte. Penn Valley Park is also home to a paved trail (just under two miles long), Washington Lake, a picnic shelter, tennis courts, a playground, a skate park, and Liberty Memorial along with the National World War I Museum. The Pioneer Mother Memorial honoring those who traveled the Santa Fe Trail through the area is in the park along with several other statues and pieces of art.

WAYSIDE WAIFS BARK PARK

You can't go to Kansas City and not take your dog to this five-acre park! Conveniently, Wayside is open twenty-four hours a day every day of the week and is located at 3901 Martha Truman Road. The park is very well maintained with shade trees, benches, covered pavilions, watering stations, and double-gated entry ways (the large-dog side for pups forty pounds and up even has a heated entry). The park sits behind Wayside Waifs Animal Shelter (a no-kill) where you can get your membership or find another loving canine companion. Daily memberships are a mere $3 (register at the front desk of Wayside Waifs during normal business hours), and members can bring a guest. All proceeds of the park go to help the shelter rescue the abused, abandoned, and homeless animals of Kansas City and the surrounding area. All dog visitors must be at least five months old and be spayed or neutered. For a complete list of park rules, go to www.waysidewaifs.org. Pay to play and help save a furry friend!

SIGHTS & EVENTS WORTH A LICK

BARK IN THE PARK

Root on the Royals with your best friend at Kauffman Stadium. This annual event is held in the spring and features pet vendors, treats with a ticket purchase, and a parade on the field. Proceeds benefit local pet adoption and rescue organizations. **Play ball!**

THE NELSON-ATKINS MUSEUM OF ART

This twenty-two-acre park boasts thirty sculptures, including the popular Shuttlecocks, which consists of several badminton birdies scattered upon the lawn. In March, the annual Dogs on the Lawn event is held here and offers paw painting, DIY doggie T-shirts, and dog art, among other fun activities. The park is just east of the Plaza and is perfect for picnicking or a **game of fetch.** Take advantage of On-the-Go Art (mobile guides) on your smart phone or check out an iPod touch at no charge.

LOVE DOGS, MUST TRAVEL: BEST OF MISSOURI

DOG RETREAT AT THE ELMS

Benefitting animal rescue, the annual Dog Retreat at the Elms is held on an August weekend and kicks off with a Friday night dog-themed movie, features numerous events on Saturday (including a fun run), and wraps up with a pancake breakfast on Sunday. Visit www.elmshotelandspa.com for information.

WALKING TOURS

Country Club Plaza is a pleasure to stroll with nearly forty pieces of art and exquisite Spanish architecture. From fountains, to unique buildings and sculptures, visitors can shop and eat amidst this fantastic and free outdoor gallery. A guide with brief descriptions of each tour stop is available at the Plaza Customer Service office at 4750 Broadway. In addition to the Plaza sights, visitors can take a walking/driving self-guided fountain tour of the city that includes over thirty fountains varying from traditional to modern design. For a more historic walking tour, download a map of Westport (www.westporthistorical.com) for twenty-five sites worth learning about. Hit the streets of the Plaza and Westport to see the fountain of Neptune, sit on Ben Franklin's lap for a great photo op, and visit Pioneer Park where a sculpture of significant historical figures—Alexander Majors, John C. McCoy, and James Bridger—now stands.

WOOFSTOCK

An annual festival for pets and people, this event benefits the Northland Animal Welfare Society (NAWS) and is held in Zona Rosa (a high-end dog-friendly shopping area) in May. Get your dog "Blessed," run the 5K or walk the mile together, enter Fido in an agility competition or fashion show, or just enjoy the entertainment and **Yappy Hour** (www.zonarosa.com/events or www.pcnaws.org).

WHERE TO SIT & STAY

THE ELMS HOTEL & SPA

Beckoning guests (including Harry S. Truman) for more than one hundred years to nearby mineral waters believed to have healing powers, the Elms Hotel & Spa has defied multiple fires and bankruptcies to continue its grand existence. Sitting upon sixteen acres of park-like grounds, the hotel has an indoor pool, a hot tub that accommodates twenty people, a volleyball court, badminton, shuffle board, and bocce ball as well as a fitness center and first-rate spa. A full-service restaurant, pub, and café are also on-site. Up to two dogs are allowed for a $50 per day fee, but each dog must be seventy-five pounds or under. Go to www.elmshotelandspa.com for descriptions of their elegant rooms and suites along with current packages. On the outskirts of Kansas City, the Elms Hotel & Spa is located at 401 Regent in Excelsior Springs—where you and your pup can **lap up luxury!**

SHERATON SUITES COUNTRY CLUB PLAZA

This hotel offers elegant and roomy two-room suites. One dog is allowed per room with a maximum weight of forty pounds with no pet fee. There is a restaurant, indoor and outdoor pool, and fitness facility on the property. Best of all, you'll be right on the Plaza, in the midst of the action.

WARRENSBURG

Approximately sixty miles from K.C., Warrensburg makes for a nice day trip where you and your pup can engage in leisurely activities during your visit. The Sensory Walkway at Blind Boone Park has a scent garden, wind harp, and water feature. World-renowned composer and pianist John William "Blind" Boone lost his sight when he was young. Visit the campus of the University of Central Missouri where you'll find over ten sculptures on display, as well as the Maastricht Friendship Tower that stands as a symbol for international understanding. Venture up Holden Street to view a mural of a 1920s downtown Warrensburg, in addition to one of Pertle Springs Resort where visitors participated in numerous outdoor activities.

Fido Fact

"Man's Best Friend"
A statue of the beloved companion and hunting dog of Charles Burden stands on the southeast corner of the Johnson County Courthouse square. Back in 1896 the black and tan hound was shot by the ward of Leonidas Hornsby (Hornsby was Burden's neighbor and brother-in-law). Drum was shot because it was believed he was the dog killing Hornsby's sheep. The case went to trial and George Graham Vest (Burden's lawyer and future senator) delivered a now-famous speech (in essence, Drum's eulogy). All those in the courthouse that day were moved by the words Vest delivered, including the term "Man's Best Friend," coined by Vest. As one of Warrensburg's most memorable citizens, Old Drum has inspired many in town to name their businesses after him. Old Drum's Memorial is at the corner of Hout and N. Holden streets, yet his burial site remains at the corner of Old Drum Road and E. 239th Street in Cass County.

SU CASA B&B

If your pup needs a bit more room to roam than a hotel can offer, then Su Casa B&B is ideal. The newly remodeled Sedona Room is available for guests with one dog, and travelers with one or more pup can stay in the Santa Fe Room. Both rooms have electric fireplaces, jet tubs, and flat-screen TVs. Guests arriving between 4-6 p.m. can enjoy a special baked snack while Fido gets his own treat along with a fresh bowl of water. There is a $20 per night per dog fee and canine visitors must be pre-approved, and not left alone. Rooms have their own private enclosed decks where you and your dog can relax outside together while enjoying the view of the resident farm animals. Both decks lead to the **dog bridge,** which takes you to the off-leash fenced dog yard where pups can run and play. Heading out to a nearby park or trail? The innkeeper will whip up a picnic lunch at your request. Visit www.sucasabb.com for a full list of amenities of this southeast Kansas City establishment, to see pictures of guest rooms, the pool, and movie room, and to learn more about this canine-welcoming ranch-style property.

THE WESTIN KANSAS CITY AT CROWN CENTER

This AAA Four-Diamond Resort is located in the heart of Crown Center and has two restaurants on-site (why not order room service?) along with Heavenly bedding, flat-screen TVs, a whirlpool, sauna, steam room, outdoor heated pool, and tennis courts. Dogs forty pounds and up are charged a $50 fee per stay and those under forty pounds are free with a signed waiver. Request a room with a balcony and view of Union Station. It's exquisite when it's snowing (www.westincrowncenterkansascity.com).

BEST BITES

BAR LOUIE

Bar Louie, awarded "Concept of Tomorrow" by *Restaurant Hospitality Magazine*, is a great place for you and your pup to chill on the patio. Known for signature martinis in addition to an extensive selection of imports, microbrews, and numerous wines offered by the glass, Bar Louie also provides consistently reliable service and delicious menu options in an eclectic atmosphere. You and Fido can visit Bar Louie at 101 E. 14th Street in the Power & Light District (see barlouieamerica.com for St. Louis–area locations). Be sure to download the Bar Louie Mobile App so you and your furry friend can send drinks to friends and receive them too!

BRIO TUSCAN GRILLE

Grab an outdoor table with your pooch and watch the city-goers on the Plaza while you sip a cool drink and savor some Italian cuisine. With an extensive menu of appetizers, flatbreads, salads, soups, pastas, steaks, and fish, it will be hard to save room for dessert. Another option is to order one of their brunch items served on weekends. Try the berries & cream French toast, crab & shrimp crepes, or one of the other delicious specialty plates from the brunch menu.

THE BROOKSIDER BAR & GRILL

The Brooksider patio offers pet-friendly dining (most of the year) along with live music, an outside bar, and TVs so you and your pup can catch the big game. Located at 6330 Brookside Plaza and open seven days a week, you'll love the food (check out the specials) and exciting atmosphere. **Paws applause!**

GORDON BIERSCH BREWERY RESTAURANT

The patio at Gordon Biersch Brewery Restaurant, where the motto is "Every Guest, Every Time," is a great location for you and your loyal companion to people watch while grabbing an award-winning lager and a delectable American dish complemented with international flavors. All menu items are made from scratch and both a vegetarian menu and a gluten-free guide are available. Don't forget to ask about the happy hour specials and beer samplers. Visit www.gordonbiersch.com for a list of tantalizing menu items and their beer history and options.

THE GRANFALLOON RESTAURANT & BAR

A happening hot spot for the locals, this fun establishment that sponsors **Dog's Night Out** often teams up with Three Dog Bakery (just around the corner) to support local canine charities. The menu has lots to offer, including the crispy shrimp rolls or mac & cheese with blue crab appetizers; the burnt end grilled cheese sandwich; Guinness beef stew; and drunken peach cobbler. Tasty fare in a fun atmosphere, this restaurant has a large patio for a perfect dining experience with your dog and is located on the Plaza at 608 Ward Parkway.

THE MIXX

For healthy food that's both fast and good, you and your four-legged friend can track an outdoor table at the Mixx. With fifty ingredients to choose from, you and Fido can create your own half or full-size salad or sandwich. He'll have to wait outside while you order inside, but your food will be delivered to your table. Better yet, call in your order and pick it up curb-side, then hightail it over to one of the nearby parks or artsy spaces in K.C. Gluten-free menu items are also available at 1347 Main Street in the Power & Light District and on the Plaza at 4855 Main Street. The Mixx is open for breakfast, lunch, and dinner.

WINSLOW'S BBQ

It would be a shame to visit K.C. without sampling some of their world-famous Q. Winslow's offers up some unique recipes with something for everyone on their menu. If you like it sweet, the bourbon bacon brisket or maple apple pulled chicken will have you licking your chops. For a real kick, order the 3rd-degree chimi laced with habañera BBQ and jalapeños, which is then deep-fried—careful not to drool! Customers can choose from pork, turkey, ham, sausage, smokie, and beef along with the traditional side items. Located at 20 E. 5th Street, customers can dine with their dogs on the patio, have Winslow's delivered, or order it to-go.

POSH PUPPY

DOGGIE STYLE BOWTIQUE

Doggie Style Bowtique is located in the historic Westport area at 1713 Westport Road. Mainly visited for their **grooming services** and self-wash station, this canine business also offers a selection of healthy food, treats, toys, other fun puppy products, training, and photography. Visit Doggie Style Bowtique any day but Monday (www.doggiestylebowtique.com).

DOG'S WORLD OF FUN

If you're in need of some **pet sitting** or your pup would prefer daycare over sightseeing, call Dog's World of Fun. In addition, this canine establishment offers grooming, training, and boarding. Go to www.dogsworldoffun.com or stop by 1220 W. 31st Street to take a look.

LAND OF PAWS

For all the latest fashion must-haves, in addition to treats, toys, and other canine needs, there's Land of Paws. Located in the northern area of Kansas City, this store provides an upscale shopping experience for you and your pup. Visit Land of Paws at 4155 N. Mulberry in Suite A or shop online at www.landofpaws.com.

THREE DOG BAKERY

Visit Three Dog Bakery on the Plaza where the smell of fresh-baked treats gets even human mouths to water. Dogs everywhere have Gracie—a deaf and partially blind Great Dane—to thank for the scrumptious snacks, quality food, and cute toys sold here. Gracie refused to eat regular food, including what the vet sent home, inspiring her loving family to create their own version of puppy chow. Their love for Gracie and other dogs led to the successful business of the bakery today, with a portion of annual proceeds going to feline and canine welfare. While you can purchase a *Three Dog Bakery Cookbook* or *Amazing Gracie* (Gracie's story) along with other products online, you and your furry friend will want to experience Three Dog Bakery firsthand. Stop in for a sweet treat and then head down the block for lunch on the patio of Granfalloon Bar and Grill. **Definitely bark-worthy!**

Jim the Wonder Dog!

A Llewellyn Setter from a line of champion field dogs, Jim was a great hunter, in addition to numerous other talents. He could decipher Morse Code, understand foreign languages, and discern both numbers and colors. Jim was featured on *Ripley's Believe It or Not*, *Animal Planet*, and the Discovery Channel. He lived to be twelve years old (in human years) and is the lone canine buried in Ridge Park Cemetery. Visitors can find a statue of Jim in the Jim the Wonder Dog Park at the northwest corner of the Square in Marshall.

NORTHWEST REGION

CHILLICOTHE

Chillicothe is the Shawnee word for "Big Town Where We Live," yet it welcomes visitors with a friendly small-town feel. With the bridge that housed the first transcontinental road in the nation, mural art galore, and the boyhood home of Walt Disney nearby, Chillicothe is home to some surprising and interesting historical facts. In addition, the town earned the title of the "Home of Sliced Bread" when the first mechanized bread slicer was used in Chillicothe in 1928. Today, guests can enjoy one of the parks in the area, participate in the Dog Daze of Summer, or soak up Chillicothe's unique history through the murals painted on buildings throughout town.

LOVE DOGS, MUST TRAVEL: BEST OF MISSOURI

PARKS & TRAILS FOR TAILS

CROWDER STATE PARK

Together, the River Forks, Redbud, and Tall Oaks trails make up seventeen-plus miles in Crowder State Park, which is north of Chillicothe in Trenton. Popular with bicyclists, hikers, fishermen, and equestrians, the park has a family-friendly campground with modern restrooms, shady picnic areas, an eighteen-acre lake, and even a tennis court. Your pup will love the endless paths among the dense forest, but with rugged terrain your pup may need protection for her paws and they should be checked often.

PERSHING STATE PARK

Pershing State Park is just east of Chillicothe and south of Highway 36. The park offers camping complete with hot showers and laundry facilities. There are several trails, but the longest is the six-mile Locust Creek Riparian Trail. Nearly a mile of the trail is an accessible boardwalk and offers interpretive signing. There is also an observation tower in the park that overlooks the largest remaining wet prairie within northern Missouri. The General John J. Pershing Boyhood Home State Historic Site, for whom the park was named, can also be found in Laclede at 1100 Pershing Drive.

SIMPSON PARK

A city landmark within Chillicothe, Simpson Park has a one-mile trail, pavilions, playgrounds, a softball field, and tennis, croquet, and sand volleyball courts. Popular with the locals for picnics, reunions, and meetings, Simpson is also home to Chillicothe's Fourth of July Freedom Festival, the annual Chillicothe Car Show, and the ever-popular Chautauqua in the Park event.

SIGHTS & EVENTS WORTH A LICK

CHAUTAUQUA IN THE PARK

Held annually in September for almost thirty years, Chautauqua in the Park is one of the most popular events of the year. An arts and crafts festival featuring musicians, all types of artwork, food, music, and children's activities provides fun for everyone. Bring Fido along to enjoy Simpson Park and a plethora of entertainment.

DOG DAZE OF SUMMER

Put your paws to the pavement and get registered for the one-mile Doggie Fun Run/Walk at the annual Dog Daze of Summer event held each July. Additionally, there is a 5K run and numerous contests and activities to enjoy afterwards. Let your pup show off his manners, showcase his talents, make a fashion statement, or enter the look-alike contest together.

DOWNTOWN WALKING TOUR OF MAIN STREET

The Downtown Walking Tour map leads visitors to seventeen murals and describes the history behind each of them. See the three-dimensional Brick Plant Mural and the two-sided Outdoor Mural, both of which are located on Elm Street. At 709 Washington Street, visitors can find the Sliced Bread Mural, which represents Chillicothe's claim to fame. Your pooch will enjoy this casual walk as you admire the artwork of Kelly Poling and try to find the names of his family members hidden in the murals. To download a map and read more about Poling, go to www.mainstreetchillicothemo.com.

LOCUST CREEK COVERED BRIDGE

The Locust Creek Covered Bridge State Historic Site sits north of Highway 36 at 16957 Dart Road in Laclede. Built in 1868, the bridge is 151 feet long and once had the nation's first transcontinental road (Route 8) running through it. Hovering above the stream below, Locust Creek Covered Bridge is a lovely piece of Missouri history and a must-see. Together, the bridge and stream make a magical backdrop for a pic of your pup while he gets a cool drink.

ST. JOSEPH

St. Joseph was founded in 1826, and visitors can see where the Pony Express began, an antique locomotive engine and historic marker (located in Patee Park), and where outlaw Jesse James spent his final days before he was shot and killed. His last house now sits at 1202 Penn Street. At Mount Mora Cemetery, you can visit the gravesites of Missouri governors, Civil War vets, Pony Express riders, and other prominent citizens while studying the architecture on the burial grounds. Visit the original Lovers' Lane and admire the beauty of Twin Spires Cathedral along with numerous historic buildings around town. Walk the twenty-six-mile parkway, which is on the National Register of Historic Places.

FOSTER'S MARTINI & WINE BAR

Located at 726 Felix, Foster's offers a spacious patio for you to enjoy food and drink with your dog in tow.

HOTELS

For those who want to make St. Joseph more than a day visit, book a room at the St. Joseph Holiday Inn Riverfront Historic Hotel or Stoney Creek Inn (both of which charge a $25 non-refundable pet fee).

LOVE DOGS, MUST TRAVEL: BEST OF MISSOURI

WHERE TO SIT & STAY

DAYS INN CHILLICOTHE

Pet-friendly and newly renovated, the Days Inn offers guests a free deluxe breakfast. All rooms have a refrigerator, microwave, pillowtop mattress, and a flat-screen TV. Some rooms have a wet bar. There is a $10 fee per pet per night but no size restriction. There is an outdoor pool and an on-site restaurant open nightly for dinner. The Days Inn is located at 606 W. Business Highway 36.

ECONO LODGE INN & SUITES

Located at 1020 S. Washington, Econo Lodge Inn & Suites has a free deluxe continental breakfast, an outdoor pool, and refrigerators and microwaves in all rooms. Rooms with hot tubs can be requested. The pet fee is a minimal $10 per night per pet with a maximum of two per room.

BEST BITES

THE BOJI STONE CAFÉ

Though there's only one table out front where you and Fido can enjoy coffee or lunch together, you can order to-go or for delivery. Wraps, grilled sandwiches, salads, quiche, pasta dishes, and even homemade desserts can be delivered between 11 a.m. and 2 p.m. in the Chillicothe area.

HICKS HOMETOWN DRIVE-IN

This fun old-fashioned drive-in serves up more than burgers and shakes. The tenderloin, BBQ beef sandwich, and frozen lemonade are popular requests, while some prefer their Mexican fare. You and Fido can order from and eat in your car or dine at one of the outdoor picnic tables at 1311 Washington Street.

NORTHEAST REGION

HANNIBAL

The mere mention of Hannibal is sure to conjure up thoughts of the mischievous adventures of Tom Sawyer and his buddy, Huck Finn. The town pays homage to Mark Twain with festivals, statues, and a park and lake named for him. You too can explore this river town just as Tom and Huck did while experiencing the places that inspired Twain's writings. In addition to celebrating the town's heritage with events such as National Tom Sawyer Days, Hannibal is home to historic B&Bs that are charming and pet-friendly, beautiful parks, and restaurants serving their guests tasty treats.

PARKS & TRAILS FOR TAILS

DEMPSEY DOG PARK

You and your pup can visit the off-leash dog park at Sixth and Ely streets. The park is open from dawn to dusk and is 1⅓ acres with separated sides for large and small dogs. There are picnic tables, shaded areas, and waste deposit stations. For a list of the park rules, visit www.hannibalparks.org.

MARK TWAIN STATE PARK

The first state park established north of the Missouri River and the third oldest in the state, Mark Twain State Park welcomes numerous visitors yet remains a peaceful getaway. Parkgoers can fish, swim, and boat in the 18,000-acre lake. Explorers will be intrigued by the park's unique flora, can observe wildlife in their natural habitat (including bald eagles), and be impressed by the view from Buzzard's Roost overlook. The Mark Twain Birthplace Historic Site sits adjacent to the park, and just west of the lake—in Paris, Missouri—is the Union Covered Bridge Historic Site (the last remaining bridge built with the Burr-arch truss system). Spend the day or set up camp (www.mostateparks.com).

RIVERVIEW PARK

Take Fido for a scenic stroll through this 465-acre park complete with picnic tables, shelters, and a playground. Follow the half-mile trail through the woods and along the river where a magnificent view of the Mighty Mississippi awaits you.

SIGHTS & EVENTS WORTH A LICK

AUTUMN HISTORIC FOLKLIFE FESTIVAL

Storytellers, street musicians, and artisans entertain visitors at this festival, now in its thirty-sixth year. Sample some wood-fired fare and grab a cup of hot apple cider as you make your way through the tents and streets of Hannibal during this 1800s-themed October event. A Midwest favorite, there's great fun for the entire family, including your furry friend. The children's area is always a big hit too.

PuppyPicks

Groomingdale's Pet Boutique
Located at 308 N. Main in the historic district, Groomingdale's is a convenient and necessary stop for you and your loyal companion. Pick up a new toy, the latest fashion item, or let your pup get freshened up. Groomingdale's also offers day camp and breed-specific merchandise.

Fido Fact

Before the moniker Mark Twain was created, the writer went by his given name, Samuel L. Clemens. Born in 1835, Clemens and his family moved from Florida, Missouri, to Hannibal when he was only four years old. His classics, The Adventures of Tom Sawyer and The Adventures of Huckleberry Finn are still studied in schools today. Aside from these popular works, he wrote A Dog's Tale (about a loyal canine and written from the dog's perspective) as well as numerous quotes, many of which were about our furry friends. Some of the more common are:

"The more I learn about people, the more I like my dog."

"Heaven goes by favor; if it went by merit, you would stay out and your dog would go in."

"It takes me a long time to lose my temper, but once lost I could not find it with a dog."

Pictures of Twain with his dog, which most believe to be some variation of the St. Bernard, are easy to find online.

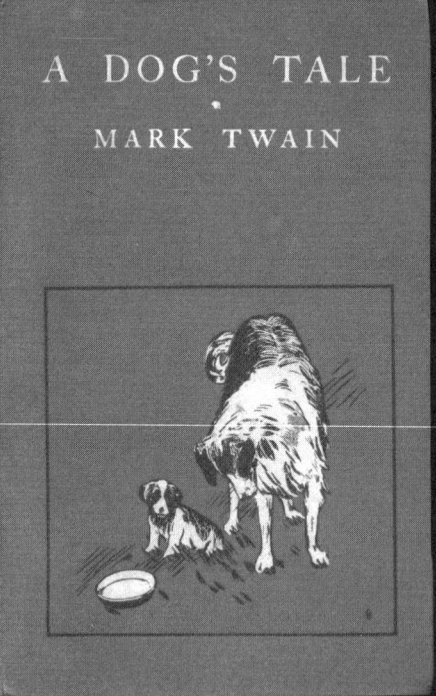

LOVE DOGS, MUST TRAVEL: BEST OF MISSOURI

LOVER'S LEAP

Lover's Leap is high atop a bluff off the Mississippi River. This five-acre park offers spectacular views of the river, Jackson Island, Hannibal, and Illinois. The park has a shelter and barbeque grill, benches, and historical information. Lover's Leap sits on the south edge of Hannibal off Highway 79 and is clearly marked.

MARK TWAIN BOYHOOD HOME

Visit the home where Mark Twain lived as a boy at 208 Hill Street. The homes of Huck Finn and Becky Thatcher are in this area, as well as the J.M. Clemens Justice of the Peace Office and Grant's Drug Store/Pilaster House. Both the Museum Gallery (featuring Norman Rockwell paintings) and the Interpretive Center are nearby.

NATIONAL TOM SAWYER DAYS

You're sure to encounter other pups at this Fourth of July celebration, as it's one of the largest festivals of the year in Hannibal. A fifty-eight-year tradition, fun-filled activities abound, such as the fence-painting competition, frog-jumping contest, mud volleyball, an arts and crafts show, live entertainment, a parade, and other Independence Day–worthy happenings. This favorite event takes place downtown and within the surrounding area. While Americans love this holiday, most canines don't love the fireworks. Be sure to check the event schedule and move on to one of the many other sights to see in Hannibal (such as the lake, where it's quiet) or take a break back at the B&B during the display. Pups have been known to get spooked and break away from their leashes only to get lost in an unfamiliar area.

WHERE TO SIT & STAY

BELLE'S PAINTED LADY

A stand-alone 1900s private home on Bird Street just off Main, the Painted Lady provides ideal accommodations for travelers with dogs who are well behaved. The property has a yard where you can walk Fido, and the enclosed sun porch offers a great view of the river where you can soak in the hot tub while your loyal companion lounges nearby. There's a king bedroom and another with twin beds, a full kitchen, living room, and a big-screen TV. Guests can walk to the historic district and Lula Belle's restaurant to enjoy a complimentary breakfast. There is **no pet fee** at this B&B (www.lulabelles.com).

HANNIBAL GARDEN HOUSE

This 1896 Queen Anne Victorian home has been in business for over ten years and has been featured on the *Today Show*. Garden House invites **well-mannered pups** to join their companions in three of their four rooms and does not charge a pet fee. There's a sunroom, an outdoor porch, seasonal gardens, cookies midday, and turn-down service. This gem is located in the historic district at 301 N. Fifth Street. Go to www.gardenhousebedandbreakfast.com to check out specials (last-minute bookings are welcomed) and to reserve your room.

BEST BITES

CASSANO'S PIZZA AND SUBS
Cassano's Pizza and Subs has the best pizza around. For delivery or to place a carry-out order, call 573-221-5442.

JAVA JIVE COFFEE HOUSE
Before you head out to explore the town where Mark Twain, Huck Finn, and Becky Thatcher roamed, stop at Java Jive for a cup of coffee to-go. With later hours than most coffee shops, you can stop by to grab one of their pastry items to enjoy back at the B&B or share an ice cream with your furry friend at one of their sidewalk tables while you watch the passersby. Java Jive is on North Main where you'll also find Ayers Pottery.

LABINNAH BISTRO
LaBinnah Bistro is just a block from Garden House B&B at 207 N. Fifth Street. This 1870 Federal-style home turned restaurant boasts fine dining in a casual atmosphere and features a lovely patio and tented area where you and your furry friend can dine together. Open Wednesday through Sunday, guests of Garden House receive a complimentary glass of wine. For entrée and wine specials, visit on Wine Up Wednesdays or Bistro Thursdays. With eclectic cuisine, top-notch service, and **Fido-friendly tables,** LaBinnah is first class! (www.gardenhousebedandbreakfast.com)

NORTHEAST REGION

KIRKSVILLE

The city of Kirksville was named after Jesse Kirk, a settler who promised dinner and free whiskey for the surveyors if they named the community for him. This college town is home to Truman State University, as well as Kirksville College of Osteopathic Medicine (KCOM), the founding location of A.T. Still University (ATSU), which has its own medicinal garden. Kirksville has been featured on the Weather Channel's *Storm Stories* as well as on Discovery Channel's *Storm Chasers*, when a 2009 tornado hit the northern edge of town. Today, the town is often referred to as the "North Star" and offers travelers spacious outdoor park areas, fun and unique festivals, and charming canine-friendly accommodations.

Fido Fact

Truman, our thirty-third president, took over the Oval Office in 1945 upon Roosevelt's death. That same year an Irish setter puppy, Mike, was given to daughter Margaret Truman by Postmaster General Robert Hannegan. She later gave him away, claiming that the staff often gave him scraps that made him ill. In 1947, the Trumans were again given the gift of a canine—a blonde cocker spaniel pup named Feller. Alas, the Truman family was not meant to have a dog. Once again they gave the pup away, this time to their physician, Dr. Graham. It is reported that when Feller was given up, it angered dog lovers nationwide. A long line of presidents have had their loyal furry friends join them at the White House where they have been seen frolicking on the lawns and greeting their companions upon the arrival of Air Force One.

PARKS & TRAILS FOR TAILS

BRASHEAR PARK

Located on West Normal Street, this park has a covered picnic shelter with electricity, a barbeque grill, a basketball court, and playground equipment. The gazebo adds to the park's beauty and serene setting. It is conveniently located for walks with your pup when staying at nearby Brashear House.

THOUSAND HILLS STATE PARK

The grounds of this 3,200-plus-acre park surround the shoreline of Forest Lake where visitors can fish, boat, ski, swim, and camp. A store with all the necessities, as well as a marina where you can rent boats, are located within the park. Trails of varying lengths offer guests several hiking options. Thousand Hills Trail can be accessed from County Road 226 and covers the less populated side of the lake. Hickory Trail covers the southern and eastern sides of the lake while passing the dam to connect to Thousand Hills Trail. Oak Trail is the shortest of the three and is nearest to picnic and shelter areas. The park is also home to a shelter that protects Native American petroglyph rocks. It is believed the area was once used as ancient ceremonial ground, and the site is listed on the National Register of Historic Places. This state park can be found at 20431 State Highway 157 (www.mostateparks.com).

SIGHTS & EVENTS WORTH A LICK

THE BACON FEST

Bring your canned goods (or a monetary donation) and pick up a free BLT to share with your furry friend at this September event held in downtown Kirksville. The event benefits the hungry within the local community. There are bacon-recipe contests such as the best entrée, healthy recipe (can you do that with bacon?), children's, and sweet dessert. Enjoy the live music, check out the kids' zone, and find out who wins the Little Miss Bacon Bits, Young Miss Sizzle, and Miss Sizzle competitions. You and Fido might even catch a glimpse of the Oscar Mayer Wienermobile. **Hot diggity-dog!**

BATTLE OF KIRKSVILLE

The 1862 Civil War Battle of Kirksville was significant, as the Union was able to claim Northern Missouri. Forest Llewellyn cemetery sits at West Washington Street and North Osteopathy, where the mass grave of Confederate soldiers is marked.

JACOB'S VINEYARD & WINERY

This six-acre family-friendly vineyard at 26078 Eagle Lane invites guests to free tastings and breathtaking views. Pups must be leashed as there are felines that call this winery home. You'll want to pack some snacks or order a picnic lunch from Steve's Garden Deli to bring along. September visitors won't want to miss Harvest Fest, where you can compete in the Grape Stomp, Bottle Corking

LOVE DOGS, MUST TRAVEL: BEST OF MISSOURI

Competition, Barrel Roll, the *I Love Lucy* Look-a-like Contest, and other activities. There's also a live band, DJ, and on-site vendors. Call 660-627-2424 for seasonal hours.

RED BARN ARTS & CRAFTS FESTIVAL

Booths filled with arts and crafts line the street of this festival, which began way back in 1974. Sponsored by the Kirksville Arts Association, proceeds help fund community arts programs. Held in September on the same weekend as Truman State University's Family Weekend, the festival is much anticipated by locals, in addition to arts and crafts enthusiasts from outside the city. Head downtown for food, dance, and musical performances; children's activities; and to see which artists are awarded monetary prizes.

TRUMAN STATE UNIVERSITY

The official school mascot, the **Bulldog,** wasn't adopted until 1915, though the school opened in 1867 and was first known as North Normal School and Commercial College. The name changed three times before becoming Truman State University in 1996. Last named for Harry S. Truman, he was the only Missourian to serve as president of the United States and ironically did not have a college degree. The school is popular for their high-quality liberal arts program, and nearly six thousand students attend Truman annually. See the quad where Baldwin Hall sat before it was destroyed by a fire (the lake that used to be here was drained while fighting the fire) and the Bell Wall built for the Centennial Celebration.

VETERANS MEMORIAL

The Adair County Veterans Memorial is dedicated to area veterans who served and sacrificed in all of our nation's battles. Located off Highway 63 in Adair County in Veterans Memorial Park, visitors can view a Civil War cannon along with a German howitzer from World War I while paying their respects.

MACON

Known for its 275,000-plus maple trees, the "City of Maples" sits about forty-five minutes south of Kirksville and is a popular destination for hunting and fishing. Dogs that like to hunt can sniff out quail, wild turkey, deer, and other forms of wildlife in the Macon area or watch you reel in the big one! See www.conservation.state.mo.us for regulations and licensing information.

Long Branch State Park is located north of Highway 36 and draws fishermen, boaters, hikers, and swimmers in addition to other visitors who want to enjoy the 1,828 acres of this outdoor haven, which consists of three areas, all of which have boat launches and picnic sites. Bee Trace was named for its popularity among early settlers searching for honey and has a nine-mile trail for pups to explore with their companions. Bloomington has a marina, store, boat rentals, fuel, swimming area, camping, and a 1.1-mile trail for less energetic canines. The Long Branch Conservation area sits on the north side of the state park where visitors can view bald eagles.

Let your pup strut his stuff in the Pooch Promenade at the Fork & Cork Festival, typically held in August. This annual event has several categories for canines and their owners, including the Best Mutt & Master where the judges look for similarities between furry and human participants, the Best Doggie Impersonators (how much do you and your dog look like a famous person or character?), and the Best Run Way Dog where high fashion is key. Ribbons are awarded to the winners at this family friendly event.

Hawg Fathers BBQ welcomes furry friends to dine with their companions on their patio and specializes in pulled pork, brisket, and ribs. They smoke their own meat, make their own sauce, and everything is made from scratch. Visit 805 N. Missouri Street for some finger lickin' good BBQ.

Well-mannered and preapproved posh pups will love the elegance, hospitality, and large yard at the Phillips Place B&B at 705 Jackson. Frugal travelers will appreciate the free breakfast, outdoor pool, and refundable pet fee (with no damage) at America's Best Value Inn & Suites (28933 Sunset Drive). While the Super 8 is also pet-friendly with a $25 fee per stay, outdoor lovers may prefer to "ruff" it at Long Branch State Park (www.mostateparks.com).

WHERE TO SIT & STAY

BRASHEAR HOUSE

Your pup will love the spacious yard, front porch, and nearby trails and parks at this 1905 Colonial B&B. Located at 1318 E. Normal Street, each elegant suite has its own private bath. There is no pet fee or size limit, but pets must be approved by the owner upon booking a room (www.brashearhouse.com). At Brashear House you'll find luxurious accommodations with Victorian flair.

COTTAGE GROVE BED & BREAKFAST

Tepr (r-pet spelled backwards) is an Australian and Norwich terrier mix and is the **resident dog** at Cottage Grove. She will share her home with other canines that are under twenty pounds. Rooms are reasonably priced and have their own private baths, refrigerators, and electric fireplaces. Travelers can request room No. 4 for access to the covered deck and yard. Fresh-baked goods, delicious meals, and fine hospitality await you at 301 S. Cottage Grove Avenue.

What Not to Doo Doo

Someone forgot to tell the city of Kirksville that there are no "bad" dogs. In any case, if you have a loyal companion with any amount of pit bull in him, you may want to bypass Kirksville altogether. Residents have specific ordinances to follow, and at the very least, visitors will need to have current records on hand showing that all immunizations are up-to-date. For clarification and the latest on city restrictions, contact the Kirksville police department at 660-785-6945. **Doggy-downer!**

NORTHEAST REGION: KIRKSVILLE

BEST BITES

MILANO'S ITALIAN RESTAURANT

Newly opened, Milano's has quickly become a town favorite. They offer fresh-baked pastas, subs, and pizza. Place an order to go or take your pup with you and dine out on the patio (which opens in summer of 2013). Call 660-627-7422 for details about their menu items and hours. Milano's Italian Restaurant is open for lunch and dinner.

STEVE'S GARDEN DELI

Located at 117 W. Washington, Steve's serves soup in lots of yummy flavors like potato bacon, as well as wraps and sandwiches, chili and **Chicago–style dogs,** lattes, dessert, and more. They even offer hot plate specials like BBQ chicken and pork loin at very reasonable prices. You'll have to order inside but staff will serve you and your loyal companion at one of the outdoor tables.

LOVE DOGS, MUST TRAVEL: BEST OF MISSOURI

CENTRAL REGION

COLUMBIA

While best known for its famous feline, Truman the Tiger, this college town is also a fan of the dog. The District—downtown Columbia's commercial district—has an exciting mix of restaurants, shopping, and art. Fenced parks, off-leash areas, and abundant trails offer canine playgrounds galore throughout the Columbia region. The numerous parks of Columbia are open to the public and visitors with no usage fees, making this city a great outdoor adventure for you and your pup to explore. Unique and seriously dog-friendly accommodations offer Fido a place to rest his weary paws and make him feel just as welcome as you will. You'll want to spend some real time in Columbia in order to experience all that it has to offer both humans and canines alike.

PuppyPicks

Trailside Café & Bike Shop
Dutch, the resident pup at Trailside, will keep your pooch company while you dine or shop at this great stop along the Katy Trail. Trailside is open April through October, but closed on Wednesdays. The shop is located at 700 First Street in Rocheport. Visit www.trailsidecafebike.com for more information.

PARKS & TRAILS FOR TAILS

COSMO PARK–BEAR CREEK NATURE AREA

Bear Creek Nature Area sits behind the skate park within Cosmo Park in northern Columbia. Fishing is allowed at the southern border on Antimi Lake, and the rolling hills will wear you and your dog out. If your dogs are like mine (easily distracted by anything that flies or is small, moving, and furry), you'll want to keep in mind that the Bear Creek Trail runs through the middle of the off-leash areas, and dogs must be leashed within fifty feet of this gravel trail. Located at 1615 Business Loop 70 West.

GARTH NATURE AREA

Another great fenced park in Columbia is located at Garth Nature Area. This off-leash dog park is approximately three acres with a pond and is a bit hilly on the west-side perimeter. There are lots of shade trees and some seating, which makes it a peaceful setting for sunny days. On the warm summer day we visited, many dogs were frolicking in the shallow water and busy chasing balls. Harlie and Kaia weren't interested in chasing balls but ran lots of large loops around the park and ate mud from the pond (mmmmm-tasty!). There were lots of people walking with their tail-wagging dogs on nearby Bear Creek Trail. One of my dogs' favorite features was the drinking fountain with pet bowl (seasonal). In all, Garth Nature Area consists of fifty-two acres and is located at 2799 N. Garth Avenue.

GRINDSTONE NATURE AREA

For a more scenic and picturesque nature walk, take your dog to Grindstone Nature Area at 2011 Old Highway 63 South. With the Hinkson Creek bordering the north and west sides and the Grindstone Creek on the east and south sides, you're sure to encounter tranquil waters where your pup can wade and get a cool drink. There are large open fields and generously wooded areas, all where your dog can run **leash-free.** Be sure to take in the scenic overlooks and make the bridge connection into Capen Park. Also popular with cyclists and climbers, this park offers something for everyone, has beautiful scenery, and shouldn't be missed!

HINKSON WOODS CONSERVATION AREA

Bordering the west side of Twin Lakes, the Hinkson Woods Conservation Area is co-managed by the Parks & Recreation and Conservation departments, and while it is not fenced, your dogs are allowed to be off-leash in the Hinkson Woods Natural History Area. For dogs like mine—with boundless energy—this is a great extension to playing at Twin Lakes. Hinkson Creek and the Katy Trail outline the boundaries of the conservation area. It can be accessed through Twin Lakes at 2500 Chapel Hill or at 2701 Forum Boulevard at the MKT access.

INDIAN HILLS PARK

At only an acre and a half, Columbia's newest fenced dog park, Indian Hills, is small compared to others in the area and is mainly used by nearby residents. However, it would be a convenient potty break stop if traveling through Columbia near the St. Charles Road/Lake of the Woods Road exit (#131) on Highway 70. A playground and swings are directly next to the off-leash area. The forty-acre Indian Hills Park also includes a basketball court, soccer and softball/baseball fields, another playground, restrooms, shelter, an 18-hole disc golf course, a grass volleyball court, and a short walking trail. It's located at 5009 Aztec Boulevard.

ROCK BRIDGE MEMORIAL STATE PARK

Rock Bridge is known for its many examples of karst topography. With caves, sinkholes, springs, and underground streams, you and your dog can spend hours hiking and exploring the natural features. A boardwalk leads hikers and their pups to the best features, including Devil's Icebox, a double sinkhole that provides visitors a view of the underground stream. Rock Bridge is located just a few miles outside of Columbia off of Highway 163. Visit http://mostateparks.com to download a map or learn more about the park.

TWIN LAKES RECREATION AREA

With so many great outdoor areas to enjoy with your dog, it might be difficult to experience them all in just one visit. Twin Lakes Recreation Area off-leash dog park is a great place to start. In summer months the area encompasses a large lake and grassy area where your dog can run and play in the water. Come winter months (the freezing time), the dog park is moved to a large sandy area nearby. While still quite large, this area has a smaller and shallower body of water to ensure the safety of our beloved furry friends. You are sure to encounter lots of friendliness here, canine and human. Twin Lakes also offers a playground and Little Mates Cove for children, a fishing dock, a shelter, four grills, restrooms, and trails and nature areas to explore. Enter at 2500 Chapel Hill Road to experience all this 73.3-acre recreation area has to offer.

SIGHTS & EVENTS WORTH A LICK

ARROW ROCK

A charming little gem of a town nestled between river bluffs, Arrow Rock is one of the oldest landmarks (the entire town, that is) on the Missouri River and is quite inviting to visitors, though less than one hundred people call it home. Part of the town is dedicated as Arrow Rock State Historic Site, which features several historic buildings and a visitors' center. Take your pup on a stroll down the streets with the self-guided walking tour. Sites include artist George Caleb Bingham's home, a country store, and trails to the river. Be sure to stop for ice cream on the boardwalk where the help is even sweeter than the ice cream. They actually came outside to ask if my pups could have a free dip! See www.arrowrock.org for tour maps.

ART IN THE PARK

Art in the Park, the largest and oldest fine arts festival in mid-Missouri, takes place at Stephens Lake Park on the first Saturday and Sunday in June. This fifty-plus-year tradition is hosted by the Columbia Art League and features the work of approximately 120 artists from around the country. This is the perfect opportunity to get outdoors with your pet before the summer gets too hot.

LIVING WINDOWS FESTIVAL

Held the first Friday of December, a quite unique kickoff to the holiday season occurs in the District. Shopkeepers perform live holiday skits for shoppers in their festively decorated display windows. Watch for Santa, the Grinch, and other holiday characters. The stories become more creative each year with merchants striving to one-up each other as carolers are heard in the background as they stroll down the streets. **Heavy-coated pups** will love the cool weather, but others might need a sweater or coat for this Christmas celebration.

PAWS IN THE PARK

Held annually in September, Paws in the Park is both a worthy and fun event for people and their pooches. Hosted by Columbia Second Chance, an organization in search of "first-class homes for second-hand pets," this event kicks off with a 5K run/walk and consists of a parade, silent auction, best-dressed and look-alike **dog contests,** demonstrations, food, and vendor and sponsor booths. It also showcases rescues from the area in need of a good home. The best part of this event is that all the proceeds go to Columbia Second Chance Adoption Center (www.columbia2ndchance.org). Take your furry friends and make a day of it.

PREHISTORIC NATIVE AMERICAN BURIAL MOUNDS

Four Hopewell Indian burial mounds, which date as far back as 100 B.C., are in Boonville, just minutes from Columbia. Three of the mounds are near Lookout Point where visitors can view the Boonslick Salt Springs and old Civil War forts of Howard County. The burial ground is located in Harley Park, which dates back to 1887 and sits on the bluffs of the Missouri River.

WALKING HISTORY TOUR OF BOONVILLE

With more than twenty points of interest on this historic walking tour, you'll find plenty to pique your interest and your pup will be glad for the walk around town. Admire the beautiful Baroque architecture of the First Presbyterian Church, visit Morgan Street Park, which features prominent Boonville figures of the past, or see the Old Jail & Hanging Barn, where the last hanging took place in 1930. You and your furry friend may also enjoy the Gas Tank Tour of Living History. Visit www.goboonville.com for additional information or to download tour brochures.

LOVE DOGS, MUST TRAVEL: BEST OF MISSOURI

WHERE TO SIT & STAY

DRURY INN

Drury Hotels are one of the most accommodating options for people traveling with their pets. Their policy allows for two pets per room with **no size limit.** The hotel kindly doesn't require a pet deposit and allows the guest to leave well-behaved pets unattended for up to thirty minutes in the room in order to indulge in the abundance of hotel amenities. Drury Hotels in Missouri are all pet-friendly and are plentiful throughout the state. The convenience and amenities of Drury make these hotels a great option for dog and cat lovers.

HOTEL FREDERICK

Dating back to 1905, this historical landmark hotel blends boutique luxury with bed & breakfast and is just steps from the Katy Trail. Rooms include robes and natural bath products, flat-screen TVs, as well as high-speed Internet access. Accommodations with Bain ultra air tubs and refrigerators are available upon request. Glenn's Café has a veranda overlooking the river and is attached to the hotel. Dogs up to seventy-five pounds are permitted, and a $25 fee covers all pets for the duration of your stay. Hotel Frederick is twenty miles from Columbia and is located at 501 E. High Street in Boonville.

LA QUINTA

Remodeled within the last few years, the La Quinta at 2500 Interstate 70 Drive Southwest is clean, bright, and conveniently located adjacent to Columbia Mall. They are one of the most reasonably priced pet-friendly options in town with rates starting under $60. There is no pet deposit or size limit, but guests are limited to two pets.

STONEY CREEK INN

You and your dog will be delighted if you're able to score one of the **pet rooms** at Stoney Creek Inn. Pet rooms were created due to the demand of travelers bringing their pets to the University of Missouri Veterinary Clinic. With potty-proof flooring, a large crate, a cot, and pet bowls provided, getting settled here is a breeze. However, there's no doubt that the best feature of the room is the door leading directly to a small patio and large grassy yard where you can walk your dog at a moment's notice. This constitutes the true meaning of dog-friendly. The rooms are complete with a refrigerator, microwave, and hypo-allergenic sheets. A stocked book shelf provides canine-friendly reading materials such as *Chicken Soup for the Dog Lover's Soul*. Weekday rates run around $110 with a $25 per pet, per night non-refundable deposit. There is a limit of two pets per room, and each is limited to no more than fifty pounds. Cats can also be accommodated with bowls, a cat box, and litter provided by Stoney Creek Inn. Stoney Creek Inn sits on the south side of Columbia at 2601 S. Providence (www.stoneycreekinn.com or 573-442-6400).

Fido Fact

Stephens College is an all-girls school that is also pet-friendly. Several of the residence halls on campus allow pets, including Tower Hall, Searcy Hall (often referred to as Pet Central), and Prunty Hall where the student-run pet fostering program is on the first floor. Finally, the perfect roommate!

BEST BITES

COFFEE ZONE

Well known for Rocket Fuel (their strong signature coffee) and the ever-changing unique soups, this Mediterranean establishment at 11 Ninth Street has a cool, laid-back vibe and eclectic décor. Salads, wraps, grill items, and desserts, including gyros and baklava, round out the menu. While there's not much seating on the sidewalk, this is a great place to get lunch to-go or hit the coffee bar for some blood-pumping caffeine.

RED MANGO

The first frozen yogurt retailer to be certified by the National Yogurt Association, Red Mango's yogurt is 100 percent all-natural, nonfat yogurt with live and active cultures. Made with fresh fruit instead of frozen and all-natural zero-calorie stevia as opposed to high-fructose corn syrup, the smoothies are amazing! You can even add an extra shot of protein. With lots of flavors and toppings to choose from, you can't go wrong, but I highly recommend the raspberry cheesecake yogurt, which got even better with every lap. Stop in 1009 E. Broadway to grab frozen treats for both you and your pup and relax at an outside table or stroll along Broadway just taking it all in.

SHAKESPEARE'S PIZZA

Not only has this establishment been named Best College Hangout by *Good Morning America*, it's been featured on *The Tonight Show with Jay Leno* and *The Late Show with David Letterman*. While that's cool and all, it's really the atmosphere and pizza that keeps customers coming back. With dough made fresh several times daily, fresh (not frozen) veggies, a sauce made from tomatoes instead of concentrate, high-grade shredded provolone, and a sausage recipe from the Hill in St. Louis, it's no surprise that Shakespeare's Pizza is considered the best pie in town. Enjoy your favorite ingredients on the patio at 225 S. Ninth Street, get it delivered, or even have one mailed to you. Shakespeare's has additional locations at 3304 Broadway Business Park Court and 3911 Peachtree Drive.

SHILOH BAR & GRILL

A local favorite, Shiloh has a roomy outdoor patio ideal for taking in some live music with your dog. Offering regular bar menu items and then some, Shiloh gives their patrons some unique choices, such as battered pickle chips (really yummy fried dill pickle slices) and Francis' BBQ salmon, a signature item. Located at 402 E. Broadway, you'll definitely want to eat here when the weather is nice and the music is jammin'.

SPARKY'S HOMEMADE ICE CREAM

A hot spot for pooches and people, Sparky's offers a wide range of flavors, such as Lavender and Honey, Les Bourgeois, Green Tea, Thin Mint Cookie, and Maple Syrup. For a twist on an adult beverage, order an alcoholic shake, float, or a Guinness topped off with a scoop of ice cream. Ask anyone in town where to go for ice cream and you're sure to get a smile and Sparky's for an answer. Stop by 21 S. Ninth Street for the best ice cream in town, but call ahead (573-443-7400) or check them out on Facebook in the colder months when their hours become seasonal.

THE UPPER CRUST BAKERY

You cannot visit Columbia without indulging at the Upper Crust Bakery on Green Meadows Way. Many local restaurants use their ingredients in their own menu items, a testament to the freshness and goodness of this restaurant and bakery. You'll find yourself drooling with desire as your eyes peruse the cases filled with decadent desserts and mini cakes (try the tiramisu), which are as pretty as they are tasty. Almost as difficult a task will be deciding what to order for lunch from a menu offering fresh salads, soups, and sandwiches. Though cozy and quaint inside, your best option is to get takeout so you can enjoy it with your dog at one of the few coveted outside tables or benches, or better yet have a picnic at one of the great parks of Columbia.

THE WINE CELLAR & BISTRO

Whether you're looking for a great glass of wine and cheeses that complement it or are hungry for a full-fledged meal, the Wine Cellar & Bistro at 505 Cherry Street is the best choice in town. While a little pricey, the food, atmosphere, and service are worth every penny. The menu offers everything from seafood to beef and chicken and even a vegetarian dish. The dungeness crab crepes are unbeatable, and the pan-seared scallops "to die for." If you just can't decide, visiting on a Sunday-Thursday allows you to create your own tasting menu with smaller portions for $30. If you thought deciding on dinner was hard, you'll really struggle with dessert. It's best to order several and share them, as they're all ooh-ahhing good. The wine list is ridiculously extensive and wine is available by the glass, bottle, and even in flights. Well-behaved canines are welcomed in the courtyard and rumor has it that a regular customer of the Wine Cellar & Bistro orders an entire entrée for her pet. **Lucky dog!**

POSH PUPPY

LIZZI & ROCCO'S NATURAL PET MARKET

Typically dogs aren't known for shopping; however, yours will love a visit to Lizzi and Rocco's Natural Pet Market on East Nifong. Owners Jessica and Kyle Schlosser started the business as a result of their passion for helping animals. According to Jessica, their emphasis is on responsible pet ownership, and they offer the highest-quality pet food and products. They work closely with local adoption agencies, especially Columbia Second Chance, and even have a small adoption program within the store. Free educational materials on pet-related topics can be found in the market along with treats, toys, supplies (grooming and otherwise), and other dog and cat products. Our favorite purchase from Lizzi and Rocco's was the **Dog Tornado,** a brain teasing toy you fill with treats. Food choices range from raw, dry, canned, and dehydrated. They even have raw meaty bones in their freezer . . . mmmmmmmm!!! While the Schlossers offer the best of the best, they also strive to keep the cost of their products reasonable.

Visit www.lizziandroccos.com for the latest on pet nutrition, in-store specials, local events and resources, health and behavioral issues, and a list of places you can adopt your next furry family member. Be sure to check out pictures of their current fosters. Warning! They're so cute you'll want to take them home.

CENTRAL REGION

FULTON

At first glance, you might easily conclude that Fulton is a sleepy little town worth passing over, but take a closer look and you'll be pulled in to all that it has to offer. While a small town, it is big in history worthy of international recognition. Fulton is engaging and charming with more than enough to pique visitors' interests. With a friendly smile and welcoming hello around each corner, Fulton has a serene feel to it, but sleepy it definitely is not! There is much to discover, and you and your furry companion will run out of daylight trying to explore all the outdoor sights, parks, and trails in the nearby area. Upon nightfall, you can rest your heads and tails at the same inn where world leaders have stayed.

No Bones About It

Saults Drug Store

Saults Drug Store on historic Court Street is not just a pharmacy. Stop in for great gift items you might typically find in a boutique, and don't leave without hitting the old-fashioned soda shop, which sits in the middle of the store. While your pup can't paw up to the counter or share a Saults milkshake with you in one of the booths, you should certainly get one to go for the two of you to indulge in as you stroll the brick streets of Fulton's historic area.

CENTRAL REGION: FULTON

PARKS & TRAILS FOR TAILS

FULTON DOG PARK

Fulton Dog Park sits just west of Business 54 and a bit off the beaten path where Brookside and Wolking drives meet. While not clearly marked on Fulton maps, the park is fairly easy to find, and your dog will certainly be glad you took the time to locate it. With two acres designated for large dogs and a half acre dedicated to small dogs, there's plenty of play area for all canine visitors. Open since 2010, the park provides shaded areas, water, and human seating. It is free and open all day. Access to the Stinson Creek Trail, a great precursor or follow up to your visit to the dog park, is across the Railroad Bridge (573-592-3190 or www.fultonmo.org).

LITTLE DIXIE LAKE CONSERVATION AREA

Just down the street from Serenity Valley Winery off Highway F, this conservation area is open year-round, and it is the perfect stop before relaxing with a Missouri wine. While the majority of the grounds are covered by forest and grasslands, there is also a 205-acre lake with fishing jetties and a dock, a boat ramp, picnic area, and pavilion. Fishing boats and canoes are available for rent. There are three trails to choose from, all classified as easy. **Dog training** is allowed in designated areas with a special-use permit. Call 573-815-7900 for specifics.

STINSON CREEK TRAIL

Meandering through streets and wooded areas, Stinson Creek Trail is a unique treat for both residents and visitors alike. Funded by contributions from the city, as well as Missouri Department of

Transportation grants, the trail boasts numerous unique landmarks such as a covered bridge, a bluff, and the Railroad Bridge, which was moved in 1902 to its current location adjacent to the off-leash dog park. At approximately five miles long with over a dozen places to access the trail, you can tailor your walk to be as long or as short as you like and to take in the sights you are most interested in exploring. Visit www.fultonmo.org to print a map of the trail to determine where you and your pooch should begin and end.

VETERANS PARK

One of the more popular parks in Fulton is located at Tenth and State streets and might be more to your liking if you prefer a lot of nearby activity or have young kids to entertain. At thirty acres, Veterans Park has a fishing lake, sand volleyball and basketball courts, a baseball field, horseshoe pits, disc golf, several playgrounds, five shelters, a skate park, amphitheater, and even an historic scout cabin. The park also contains the Blue Star Memorial, a tribute to the U.S. Armed Forces.

WALLACE BACKER PARK

For those of you who feel overwhelmed just hearing about all that Veterans Park has to offer, Wallace Backer Park might be a better choice for you. You and your dog can hike the 5.5 acres of this undeveloped nature area while enjoying the peaceful calls of the wildlife that roam here. Get back to nature in this hilltop park that was donated to the city in 2009 by the Fulton Garden Club.

SIGHTS & EVENTS WORTH A LICK

NATIONAL CHURCHILL MUSEUM

The National Churchill Museum sits upon the campus grounds of Westminster College (where Churchill gave his famous Iron Curtain speech in 1946), along with "Breakthrough" (see page 46) and St. Mary's Church. Sir Winston Leonard Spencer Churchill wore many hats. Some of his many hats included writer, British army officer, artist, **dog lover,** and politician/statesman during World War II. As the first person to earn the title of honorary citizen of the United States and the only British prime minister to receive the Nobel Prize in Literature, Churchill was well respected and had many roles throughout his life that are documented extensively within the museum through permanent and temporary displays. The museum is open daily (except for a few holidays), and admission for Westminster students as well as Callaway County students is free. Other tickets range from $3 to $6. Dogs are not allowed inside the structures but can wander the campus grounds to experience Churchill's legacy. Take a moment to reflect by the fountain in the quiet English Garden that sits just to the right of the museum entrance and the bust of Winston Churchill as he warned the world that "an iron curtain has descended across the continent."

SERENITY VALLEY WINERY

Just the drive in on the winding gravel road through fields of wind-blown farm grasses calms the spirit, and you immediately understand why the word "serenity" is part of this winery's name. Regina Ruppert and her husband, Lee, moved their establishment from O'Fallon, Missouri, to this more peaceful setting in 2011, and business has thrived ever since. They have numerous canine visitors and even offer a wine called the Perfect Pear (only for human consumption, of course) featuring their own two French bulldogs on the label. Wine tasting is complimentary, and gifts, cheese trays, and appetizers are available for purchase. Beer is also available, and employees at Serenity Valley have been known to bring out fresh water for pups. Uniquely, Serenity Valley Winery accommodates those who want to make and bottle their own wine and will even help you create a personal label. The facility can accommodate twenty guests indoors (sorry, pups have to remain outside) and an unlimited number outside for private parties. Observe the craft of wine-making, sit back, and gaze at the lake while you sip a flavorful boutique wine, or spend a warm summer evening here with Fido and friends. Serenity Valley Winery sits just on the outskirts of Fulton at 1888 County 342 in Millersburg, near the intersection of state highways J, F, and WW. Depending on which direction you're coming from, it's possible to miss the sign, and calling ahead for detailed directions is recommended (573-642-6958).

BERLIN WALL AND "BREAKTHROUGH"

Standing just west of the Churchill Museum in front of the Church of St. Mary is "Breakthrough," the thirty-two-foot long and eleven-foot tall sculpture created with eight actual pieces of the Berlin Wall by Winston Churchill's granddaughter, Edwina Sandys. She purposely chose the pieces that were scarred with much colorful graffiti, including the word "*unwahr*," meaning lies or untruth to those Germans held back by the wall. Personally dedicated on November 9, 1990, by President Ronald Reagan, the sculpture can be physically touched and walked through by visitors. Snap a quick pic as your dog passes through for a great keepsake of your trip to Fulton. This piece of art represents the men and women who broke through the wall to find freedom on the other side.

CHURCH OF ST. MARY THE VIRGIN, ALDERMANBURY

The Church of St. Mary is attached to the rear of the museum and once stood in London, having survived World War II. After Winston Churchill's visit to there, her pieces were flown to Fulton and the church was reconstructed as a way to memorialize Churchill. President Harry Truman turned the symbolic first shovel on April 19, 1964, and a little over five years later, on the day of the dedication, a crowd of 10,000 gathered for the celebration. The ceremony was attended by Churchill's youngest daughter, a member of the Royal Family, the Queen's Representative, and many other prominent figures of England. Tours of the church are available with the museum; however, it may not be open on days when weddings and other special events are being held. Your pup will be happy to

Fido Fact

Animal lover Winston Churchill once said, "Dogs look up to you, cats look down on you. Give me a pig. He just looks you in the eye and treats you as an equal." While he may have seen swine as equal, it was cats and dogs that were his house pets. Churchill had an orange cat named Jock, numerous strays, and Nelson (named for Lord Nelson) who was known to sit in a chair next to him in the cabinet and dining rooms. While Nelson helped Churchill with his business affairs, it seems that his black poodle, Rufus, was the one who was really living the good life. No one ate dinner until the butler served Rufus his meal, placed upon the Persian carpet near Churchill in the dining room where the rest of the family also ate. Rufus often accompanied his owner to Chequers to watch movies. Right before the scene in Oliver Twist in which Bill Sikes is about to drown his dog, Churchill covered Rufus's eyes to spare him from the pain. He told Rufus, "Don't look now, dear. I'll tell you about it afterwards." Unfortunately, Rufus did not have nine lives and after his death was replaced with another black poodle, named Rufus II.

enjoy the lush grassy area with fountains in front of the church while you rest on one of the benches and admire the beauty of this historic seventeenth-century structure. For all things Churchill, visit www.national-churchillmuseum.org.

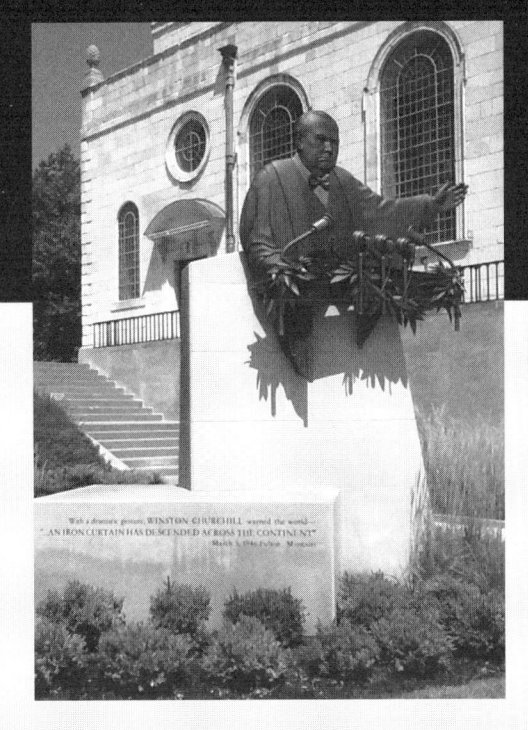

CENTRAL REGION: FULTON

WHERE TO SIT & STAY

HOLIDAY INN EXPRESS

While it's no comparison to Loganberry Inn, the Holiday Inn Express is conveniently located off Highway 54 at 2205 Cardinal Drive and a good Plan B. A reasonable fee of $25 a dog with no size or number limit, this hotel is a viable option for travelers with pets. Dogs are not allowed to be left unattended in rooms, so be sure to bring a traveling companion that can stay with him so you can take a dip in the pool, soak in the hot tub, or hit the fitness center. Along with a hot complimentary breakfast, the Holiday Inn Express serves cookies, ice cream, or popcorn nightly and has an unlimited cocktail hour and free appetizers on Wednesday nights. Pet rooms are standard with either a king or two double beds and are limited in quantity. All pet rooms feature a mini-fridge, microwave, coffee maker, and a flat-screen television. Go to www.holidayinn.com to book a room.

LOGANBERRY INN

Within walking distance of the Westminster campus is Loganberry Inn, an 1899 grand Victorian and *the* place to stay in Fulton. Loganberry Inn has welcomed past guests like Margaret Thatcher, a Nobel Peace Prize winner, and family of Winston Churchill. Today, inn owners Cathy and Carl McGeorge welcome travelers from all over the country, both human and canine. They aim to please and definitely hit their mark. Logan, a confident Shi Tzu, is the resident greeter and swift to welcome visitors. The Garden Room boasts all the modern conveniences of home: a fireplace, comfy king bed with extra pillows, a beverage center with coffee and tea, a small table and chairs, plus two recliners in front of a flat-screen. Harlie and Kaia would argue that the best thing about the Garden Room is that it conveniently has its own exit leading to the fenced backyard. Logan will be happy to show canine visitors around and engage in some fun puppy play. Cathy is a gourmet cook and whips up an indulgent breakfast that would be sinful for guests to miss! Also available to travelers with dogs, the Winston Churchill room is the original library of the home and conveniently located by the front entrance for quick puppy potty breaks. There is a limit of two dogs per room, a $15 fee, and some restrictions may apply. Go to www.loganberryinn.com for all the details and to book a stay for yourself and Fido.

CENTRAL REGION: FULTON

BEST BITES

ARRIS' PIZZA
Show *eros* for your dog and order an Arris' specialty pizza to-go, to eat in one of the beautiful park settings around town. While it's hard to pass up one of the numerous pies named after a Greek God, Arris' also offers a wide selection of other items of both Greek and American variety. Choose from a lengthy list of appetizers, salads, subs and other sandwiches, pastas, and even steak or salmon. Be sure to indulge in a piece of baklava, a Greek favorite, or order a piece of cheesecake for later. Arris' Pizza is located at 61 W. Second Street across from Veterans Park with additional locations in Jefferson City, Columbia, Osage Beach, and Springfield.

What Not to Doo Doo

Hit the Bricks
With the "Hit the Crik" Crawdad Eating Contest, live music, a parade, and tons of booths lining the street, one would think that the Fulton Street Fair in June would be loads of fun for the whole family. And it is, just not for canines anymore. Once enjoyed by our furry friends too, an unfortunate non-canine incident occurred, forcing local officials to put a ban on the festivities for dogs. Someone always has to stink it up for the rest of us!

LOVE DOGS, MUST TRAVEL: BEST OF MISSOURI

CENTRAL REGION

HERMANN

Picturesque and perched along the Missouri River, Hermann boasts Old World charm and sets the tone for peaceful moments from the minute you cruise in off the rolling hills that lead you to this quaint German settlement. Established back in 1837, Hermann is best known for being "wine country," and people come from all over the state for tastings and just to enjoy the views of the countryside and vineyards. While wine is the most popular "event" in town, Hermann is also known as the "Sausage Capital of Missouri," which it celebrates each March with the Wurstfest. Aside from sipping wine, there's plenty to do and see while visiting, such as partaking in the local festivals and visiting historic sites. Of course, there's no shortage of places to purchase all the local favorite wines and snacks to take along with you for adventures with your pup.

PARKS & TRAILS FOR TAILS

HERMANN CITY PARK

As host to the BarBQ & Brats Festival, as well as other local events, and with a walking tour dedicated to it, this park is a popular outdoor space in Hermann. Easily found at 1902 Jefferson Street, the park also offers camping with everything from primitive to RV and group sites with full hookups. There is a playground, outdoor pool, and bicycle rentals, as well as a bathhouse. The campground is open year-round, has minimal fees, and leashed dogs are welcome. The park is a great place for a leisurely walk with your pup, and the City Park Walking Tour is definitely worthwhile.

THE KATY TRAIL

A perfect opportunity to burn off some energy with man's best friend, the section of the Katy Trail near Hermann offers gorgeous views of vineyards and peaceful scenic paths. Make a day of it and picnic along the way or start your day off with a short hike to sate your pup before enjoying the town. You're sure to see others on the trail as Hermann is a popular spot to stop for those traveling the Katy. For additional information, pick up a copy of *Katy Trail Guidebook* by Brett Dufur. If you're lucky enough to be staying at the Apfelbaum, there is a copy in the cottage. It's worth perusing.

SIGHTS & EVENTS WORTH A LICK

BARBQ & BRATS FESTIVAL

This late-September event takes place in the City Park and features lots of (you guessed it) barbeque and brats. There are numerous competitions to see whose "que" is the best, including one for kids. Bring your dog and a chair (as seating is limited) and take in the live entertainment, visit the wine and beer garden, or enter your recipe for a cash prize. There is a small fee of $5 per person for entry to the event, and those 12 and under get in free.

HERMANN WURSTFEST

This annual event is held in late March and has been honoring sausage for over three decades now! Activities are scheduled in numerous locations around town, but your pup will be most interested in the canine happenings that take place in City Park. Included in the celebration are the **wiener dog talent show,** a costume contest, and races. Pups as young as 16 weeks are allowed to enter the Cocktail Franks division, with Frankfurters being for 6 months to 5 years, and finally, 5 years and older are entered in the Ballpark Franks division. This is the perfect opportunity for your four-legged friend to show those bigger dogs that short legs can move fast too, show off her fashion sense or make his talent known to all. Don't have a wiener dog? Then take your pup down to the park to cheer on your favorite competitors. There is a minimal fee to enter the contests, with a discount for registering early. Go to www.visithermann.com/special_events/wurst for a schedule or to register your wiener dog.

MAIFEST

The Maifest tradition, which celebrates the last day of school, first began sometime in the early 1870s after the first German school was built in Hermann. Children dressed in their Sunday best and after dinner and church played games and ate knockwurst, popcorn, and candy. Today, on the third weekend of May, locals and tourists alike celebrate spring with games, a parade, and visits to the wine and beer gardens in Sesquicentennial Park or Hermann City Park. Of course, there's German music and dancing, as well as traditional German food. Events take place at different locations throughout town. Check www.visithermann.com/special_events/maifest for this year's schedule.

OKTOBERFEST

With its German heritage, Oktoberfest is the most anticipated celebration of the year in Hermann. Held on the first four weekends in October, the spectacular colors of fall enhance the already stunning views from the high bluffs and hilltops. Most of the wineries host live music acts, and Sesquicentennial Park has the ever-popular Bier Garten, traditional festival and German food, and live entertainment.

Hosted by the Gasconade County Historical Society, the annual Hermann City Cemetery Walk is a unique activity that takes place during Oktoberfest. Several characters from days gone by will meet you at their gravesite in period clothing and tell you their own personal story and connection to the town. Tickets for the walk are just $10.

OktoberTour

LOVE DOGS, MUST TRAVEL: BEST OF MISSOURI

WALKING TOURS

The walking tours are a great way for you and your pup to explore the German riverfront town of Hermann by foot and paw.

THE BAYER WALKING TOUR

This tour is named for George Bayer, who was commissioned to purchase land for settlers coming to Hermann. Notable sites are the Tin Mill Brewery (the first commercial brewery in town since Prohibition), Sesquicentennial Park where many festivals are held, the Old Catholic Cemetery, and the Hermann Farm Stable and Wagon Works area. Walking tours are self-guided, and visitors can pick up maps at 312 Market at the Welcome Center.

THE CITY PARK WALKING TOUR

The City Park Walking Tour starts at the Rotunda, which was built in 1864 and is on the National Register of Historic Places and was also put on the list of Missouri's Ten Most Endangered Historic Places in 2005. Other stops include the Charles Eitzen Memorial, dedicated to the park founder; Stone Hill Winery, where dogs are allowed on the outside of the property; the mansions of both of the original owners of Stone Hill, Stark Mansion (Stark's Wine Castle) and Birk's Gasthaus/Herzog Mansion (now a B&B).

THE RIVERFRONT WALKING TOUR

The highlights of this riverfront tour include the White House Hotel, which has accommodated famous guests like Ty Cobb; the Lewis and Clark Marker; and the Hermann Star Mill, which was the first steam-powered grist mill in Hermann.

WHERE TO SIT & STAY

APFELBAUM COTTAGE

Owners of Apfelbaum Cottage and their dog, Buddy, designed this home to be not only kid-friendly but accommodating to Fido too! The property is located in the center of town at 138 W. Fifth Street and is just blocks from both City Park and the Katy Trail. Your pups will be grateful for the fenced yard where they can sniff things out while you barbeque or just relax with a bottle of wine you picked up from one of the nearby wineries. With a leather pull-out sofa and separate bedroom with a queen bed, the cottage is cozy yet large enough to accommodate up to four people. The eat-in kitchen is stocked with all the utensils you'll need, including wine glasses, and the flat-screen TV, DVDs, and WiFi allow you and your pup to snuggle up together for some down time after exploring the heritage of Hermann. Nightly, weekend, and weekly rates are offered, and conveniently there is a discounted rate for guests that do not use the pull-out sofa for sleeping. Rates start at $145 nightly but drop considerably for weekly stays. There is a $20 pet fee per dog by the night, and the weekly charge is just under $15 per pet. The cottage books well in advance for Oktoberfest and other local events so be sure to reserve this gem early. Go to www.apfelbaumcottage.com for rates and additional information.

HERMANN HILL

Hermann Hill, an elegant inn boasting luxurious accommodations, sits atop the high bluffs overlooking the winding Missouri River and offers two canine-friendly options. Both rooms have see-thru fireplaces, jacuzzis, and spa-like showers and include a delicious homemade breakfast. Village Riverbluff Cottage #502 is on the lower level and is easily accessible to an exercise area. The Vidal is located within the inn and has a patio and private access to a three-mile walking path that will have your dog barking for joy. One dog under thirty pounds is allowed with a $50 non-refundable cleaning fee. Dogs are not permitted to be left unattended or on the beds, and rooms are inspected prior to the guest's departure. Visit the website for pictures of accommodations, special packages, and other amenities offered at Hermann Hill. In addition, you can call on Mondays and Thursdays for last-minute deals (www.hermannhill.com or 573-486-HILL).

BEST BITES

ESPRESSO LAINE AT THE JUNCTION

For the perfect blend of coffee, smoothies, cappuccinos, or lattes, stop by the Junction at 407 E. First Street. Homemade pastries should not be passed up, and you might even want to select some fresh beans to brew at the cottage or inn later. Sandwiches and fruit are available for lunch at this downtown treasure. With several outdoor tables on the wrap-around porch, this is a great place for you and your furry friend to have lunch, or just reenergize with a midday jolt of caffeine.

HERMANN WURST HAUS

Located at 234 E. First Street, Hermann Wurst Haus has about every variety of sausage (over forty between the sausage and brats sold here), cheese, wine, and beer that you could want. This is an ideal place to pick up lunch to-go from the deli or a cheese plate to soak up the wine you know you are going to be sipping on later. Hermann Wurst Haus is open every day of the week and features Amish products, provides mail order, caters, and sells gifts. Be sure to stop in to see all that this one-stop shop has to offer.

JILLSIES

A unique selection of gifts (think luxurious goat's milk soaps, lotions, toys, and clothes) and a menu of coffees, smoothies, salads, sandwiches, appetizers, and pastries sets Jillsies apart from other eateries in town. Grab a sandwich and frappe to-go and lunch with your pup at the City Park or by the riverfront. Jillsies sits at 201 Schiller Street and is closed on Mondays.

RICKY'S CHOCOLATE BOX

Soothe your sweet tooth and pick up a heavenly piece of chocolate to indulge in later or for the perfect addition to your wine. If you can dream it, they've made it. From turtles to pretzels to truffles to clusters in every flavor imaginable, you'll want to order some specialty chocolate too. Sorry, Fido! This is one treat you can't have. Stop in at 310 Market Street or order online at www.rickyschocolatebox.com.

TRAILSIDE BAR & GRILL

With daily specials at around $5, fried chicken, catfish, weekend barbeque, and hearty breakfasts on the menu, you can't go wrong ordering something to-go from the "Corner" (as the locals call it). Across from the Katy Trail at 111 Bluff, this restaurant is ideally located for early morning hikers and cyclists rolling in later in the evenings, and has quite the reputation for not only good food but a friendly atmosphere too.

WINERIES

Wineries abound in Hermann. Below are some of the best options to enjoy with your pup.

ADAM PUCHTA WINERY

Located in Frene Creek Valley, this winery happens to be one of the few within the United States to still be owned and operated by the original family since its beginning in 1955. With large outdoor areas for you and your pooch to roam and too many awards to mention, Adam Puchta Winery is open seven days a week, but closed on major holidays. Take your wine and provisions from the country store and find your hillside spot to take in the sunset or cozy up to the fire pit on cooler days. Dogs on leashes are welcome; however, they should be appropriately behaved around felines, as many cats call this winery home.

HERMANNHOF WINERY

Opening in 1852 in the French section of Hermann, this establishment was originally more brewery than winery. It is conveniently located at 330 E. First Street in the heart of downtown and is on the National Register of Historic Places. The large outdoor patio lets you enjoy lunch with your furry friend while watching the busy streets of this charming town. Sausage, cheese, wine, gift items, and souvenirs are available for purchase in the winery's store.

STONE HILL WINERY

Order something wonderful off the menu from Vintage Restaurant (located at Stone Hill), grab a bottle of wine (to cleanse the palate of course), and head out to the grassy hill with your furry friend to take in the mesmerizing view that overlooks the charming town of Hermann. The restaurant offers everything from small plates and entrees to German food and dessert. During Oktoberfest and other celebrations, you and your pup can enjoy the live music at the pavilion, in addition to the breathtaking view of the village below. Try one of Stone Hill's numerous award-winning selections and see for yourself why it is thriving after 160 years in the wine-making business.

CENTRAL REGION

JEFFERSON CITY

Named after Thomas Jefferson, a Founding Father and the third president of the United States, Jefferson City is home to Missouri's State Capitol and sits directly on the Missouri River. The state capital was relocated from St. Charles in the 1820s in order to be more centrally located along the river between Kansas City and St. Louis. Prior to that time, Jefferson City was only a trading post and simply known as Lohman's Landing. The Jefferson Landing, now a State Historic Site, is a rare surviving Missouri River landing. The Charles Lohman Building was built there in 1839 and used as a hotel, store, and warehouse. In addition, living quarters for the wharf master and headquarters for the steamboat company were located in this building. The building still stands today at 100 Jefferson as a visitor's center, for those who want to take a peek into our state's past. While you would have to know someone pretty high up to get your dog a tour of our State Capitol, there's an abundance of historic sites and other exciting things to see and do on your own while visiting this city, many of which are best visited on paws and by foot.

PARKS & TRAILS FOR TAILS

CENTRAL MISSOURI MASTER GARDENERS' DEMONSTRATION GARDENS

The Children's Garden of aromatic and sensory plants is just one of the five connecting gardens that were co-created by the Master Gardeners and Parks & Recreation. Take a moment to wander the paths that lead to a Native American Medicine Wheel, a River's Edge overlook, or the Kitchen Garden where heritage vegetable plants and herbs are grown. The Master Gardeners continue to maintain the park, and varieties of flowers and plants are constantly changing. You and your furry friend should definitely take time to smell the roses in the Memorial Rose Garden—a true original (www.jeffcitymo.org/parks).

MISSOURI RIVER PEDESTRIAN AND BIKE BRIDGE

With two lookout points, the Missouri River Pedestrian and Bike Bridge provides you and your pup another outstanding view of the State Capitol, as well as Jefferson City's riverfront. This newer extension to the Highway 54 Missouri River Bridge allows pedestrians and bikers (including those coming from the Katy Trail) convenient access between the northern part of the city into the heart of it. The pedestrian bridge stretches a generous eight feet wide and is ADA accessible. For additional information about the bridge, call 573-632-2820.

NORTH JEFFERSON CITY DOG PARK

The North Jefferson City Dog Park provides an area for canines to run and play off-leash and is located in the recreational area at 810 Sandstone Drive. The large-dog park is for dogs over thirty pounds, but it has a side for the lightweights. The park has a double-gated entrance, park benches, a water source, and waste disposal stations. While the park is primarily used by local residents, visitors can easily obtain a usage permit for their stay. To apply for the permit, visit the Parks & Recreation Department at 427 Monroe Street during normal business hours of 8 a.m. to 5 p.m. Monday through Friday. Visitors will be required to provide their pet's current vet records to show that all vaccinations are up-to-date and to register their dog. After paying a pro-rated amount of $2 a month, Parks & Recreation will provide a receipt to carry with you while visiting the park. The North Jefferson Recreation Area encompasses 165 acres and also includes a one-mile trail that connects to the Katy Trail, access to the Missouri River with a boat ramp, a picnic shelter, and a pavilion. For a list of park rules, to obtain additional information, or to apply for a permit prior to arriving in Jefferson City, contact Parks & Recreation at 573-634-6482 or go to www.jeffcitymo.org/parks.

SIGHTS & EVENTS WORTH A LICK

CAPITAL JAZZFEST

Once a year in September for over twenty years now, Jazz Forward Initiative and other non-profits have lured Missourians to the downtown streets of High and Madison with a collaboration of jazz and blues. Performers come from all over the region to play in the hopes of preserving the appreciation of jazz music. This cultural event is free and coincides with the Capital Street Art Fair, where the medium is chalk.

DOWNTOWN AUDIO/VIDEO WALKING TOUR

Stop by the Jefferson City Convention and Visitors Bureau at 100 E. High Street and grab an mp3 player and a downtown walking tour brochure before you and your pup head out to admire the architecture and sights of the state capital city. Go to www.jeffcitymo.org/parks/downtownfitnessmile.html and download the Downtown Fitness Mile Map for an abbreviated self-guided walk. The historic tours booklet will also come in handy for walking or driving tours of historic churches and homes, the State Capitol grounds, Civil War sites, and other historical buildings.

LOVE DOGS, MUST TRAVEL: BEST OF MISSOURI

LEWIS AND CLARK TRAILHEAD PLAZA

The Lewis and Clark "Corps of Discovery" Commemorative Monument is just east of the State Capitol. The five bronze figures were created by sculptor Sabra Tull Meyer, and Austin Tao Associates of St. Louis designed the waterfall and limestone plaza area. The efforts of both combined make for a truly beautiful setting that overlooks the Jefferson Landing State Historic Site. The monument features not only Meriwether Lewis and William Clark, but also the dog Seaman (my pups' favorite historical figure of Missouri), George Drouillard, and York, Clark's enslaved servant. The monument is quite accessible, enabling visitors to walk right up to the figures. From May through September, docents present information about the expedition and the personalities of all the figures featured in the monument. Visit www.jeffcitymo.org/parks/LCIndividualVisitorPrograms.html for specific days and times. Adjacent to these statues is a three-tier water fountain, with the lowest tier at almost ground level for dogs to quench their thirst. It's a great photo op for you and your dog!

GOVERNOR'S MANSION AND STATE CAPITOL

Although neither the Missouri State Capitol nor the Governor's Mansion allow dogs inside—unless it's the first dog, of course—both sites are essential to a visit to Jefferson City. The Capitol has extensive grounds to explore with your dog, and there are sites surrounding it. Built in 1917, the Capitol rises 238 feet above ground level and dominates Jefferson City. The exterior of the Governor's Mansion, designed by noted architect George Ingham Barnett in the Second Empire style, is impressive enough to pay a visit. The mansion is a short walk from the Capitol near the Amtrak station and the Jefferson Landing State Historic Site on the riverfront.

Fido Fact

First Dog Daniel Boone, a Welsh springer-spaniel, moved into the governor's digs with his parents—Governor Jay Nixon and First Lady Georganne Wheeler Nixon—in 2009 after Governor Nixon took office. Boone, for short, frequently takes time out from his busy dog days to appear at events and on tours, as well as some important dinners on the mansion grounds. Boone's birthday is April 1.

LOVE DOGS, MUST TRAVEL: BEST OF MISSOURI

WHERE TO SIT & STAY

CAPITOL PLAZA HOTEL

Conveniently close to many popular attractions in the heart of Jefferson City, this non-smoking, pet-friendly hotel is located downtown at 415 W. McCarty Street and is a perfect choice for either work or pleasure trips. Pets are allowed in any of the rooms (well-behaved dogs may be left alone), and a non-refundable $20 fee covers any size and number of dogs. Be sure to request a junior or king suite if you'd like a refrigerator, microwave, or sofa sleeper in your room. Park Place restaurant and the Fountain Court Lounge are both on-site, as well as an indoor pool and whirlpool, fitness center, business center, and a 24-hour gift shop. One-day dry cleaning, free WiFi, and parking are also offered. Be sure to refer to www.capitolplazajeffersoncity.com for current specials and packages. This modern and attractive hotel has AAA 3-Diamond and Mobil 3-Star ratings and has everything that your dog (and you) will need during your stay. Be sure to book the Presidential Suite if your dog is feeling stately!

TRUMAN HOTEL & CONFERENCE CENTER

The Truman Hotel & Conference Center is located off Highway 54 (1510 Jefferson Street) and offers a complimentary hot breakfast Monday through Friday, an outdoor pool and patio, exercise room, free parking, and business services along with high-speed wireless Internet. Guests of the hotel can even get four complimentary movie tickets to the adjacent Truman 4 Theaters. Bingham's (named after Missouri artist George Caleb Bingham and well known for its popular Sunday brunch) and the Library Lounge offer guests convenient meals and cocktails. A minimal pet fee of just $10 is required per night with no limit on number or size of dogs per room. However, all pets must be kenneled if you are leaving them in the room alone. McKay Park and walking trails are nearby to accommodate your pup. Rooms are elegantly furnished and quite reasonably priced. According to the staff, the general manager is a breeder and **dog lover,** so Fido is sure to feel welcome.

BEST BITES

CAFÉ VIA ROMA

Café via Roma invites customers to indulge in "a taste of Europe in the Capitol City" right here in the Midwest. The intoxicating aroma of fresh-ground beans paired with a relaxed vibe entices visitors to just settle into the moment. The menu offers coffee and non-coffee specialty drinks, breakfast items, panini sandwiches, wraps and croissants, gourmet salads, pastas, and fresh-baked goods and desserts. Look for the sidewalk tables with orange umbrellas just down from the State Capitol at 105 W. High Street. For a complete list of menu items go to www.cafeviaroma.com.

CAPITOL CITY CORK & PROVISIONS

Grab an outdoor table and unwind at Jefferson City's best and newest American wine bar at 124 E. High Street. The definition of *provisions* is "to supply with food and drink," which the owner of Cork does splendidly. The menu offers a wide selection of ever-changing wines, soups (the Hungarian mushroom is unbeatable), salads, sandwiches, desserts, pastas, and lots of other really yummy stuff. Whether you just want to relax with some wine and cheese after taking in the sights of our capital city or want to hang at the hottest spot in town, Cork is the place to go. Find them on Facebook for pictures of their latest creations and delicious dishes.

MADISON'S CAFÉ

Known for elegant yet casual Italian dining, Madison's has long been a favorite of locals and visitors alike. You can still have the best of both worlds (great food and great company) while dining out with your dog at one of their elegant outdoor tables (take-out is also available if visiting during colder months). Their mouth-watering menu offers an abundance of pasta dishes (including light fare and gluten-free options), numerous seafood items, and an extensive list of choice cuts of beef, soups, salads, and sandwiches along with delectable desserts and a never-ending wine list. In 2012 the restaurant added an epicurean Small Plates Menu for Happy Hour Monday through Friday. Appropriately, Madison's Café sits at 216 Madison. Visit www.madisonscafe.com to see what's new on the ever-changing menu.

YANIS COFFEE ZONE

Known for friendly service and scrumptious menu items made with fresh local products, this coffee house and Mediterranean grill is a popular stop for many downtown workers and an excellent choice for you and your dog. This establishment offers an array of soups, sandwiches (the gyros breakfast sandwich is a local favorite), hummus, and other menu items that you can enjoy at a sidewalk table or nearby park with your furry friend. Rumor has it that once you try their bold Turkish-style coffee, you'll be hooked. Experience it for yourself at 130 E. High Street.

ZESTO

For a good old-fashioned foot-long dog, milkshake, or other traditional drive-in menu items, visit Zesto-South at 1730 Jefferson Street. In business since 1948, it offers lots of tasty treats, including numerous award-winning barbeque options. While not actually a drive-in (you have to order inside at the counter), you can enjoy all your favorite treats with your pup at one of their outside tables where you can still catch a glimpse of the State Capitol.

CENTRAL REGION

LAKE OF THE OZARKS

One of Missouri's premier vacation spots, Lake of the Ozarks is brimming with activities for you and your dog. The lake covers over 54,000 acres and has more than 1,100 miles of shoreline. Every water activity imaginable can be found. However, there are many land attractions to enjoy like state parks, as well as the Canine Cannonball, which is specifically geared toward our furry friends! As the largest manmade lake in the Midwest (its water levels are maintained by Bagnell Dam, which separates it from the Osage River), the lake area encompasses numerous communities. Whether you and your four-legged friend are adventurers, the boating type, or are just looking for some R&R, the lake is a great place to visit.

Photo courtesy Lishia Moore

PARKS & TRAILS FOR TAILS

BARK PARK

Located off Horseshoe Bend Parkway in the Four Seasons community, this one-acre off-leash park is available for anyone's use and is open twenty-four hours a day year-round. The water source, wading pool, and trash service are donated by local businesses, and guests are encouraged to make a monetary donation to help maintain the park. This is the only off-leash park in the area and is conveniently located near pet-friendly lodging.

HA HA TONKA STATE PARK

The centerpiece of the 3,600-acre Ha Ha Tonka State Park is the burned-out ruins of a European-style castle that sits atop a bluff. While the castle was being built, the owner was killed in a car accident, which left his sons to complete the remainder of the structure. Once completed, it was leased to a lady who used it as

Photo courtesy Matt Hambly

LOVE DOGS, MUST TRAVEL: BEST OF MISSOURI

a hotel until it was destroyed by fire in 1942. After the fire, and over thirty years later, the state of Missouri purchased the property and made it a state park for the public to enjoy. The park sits on the Niangua Arm of the Lake of the Ozarks and on State Road D, a few miles southwest of Camdenton. With twelve trails that vary in length and total sixteen miles, you and your pup can enjoy the great outdoors while getting some exercise. The park is also home to eight known caves, one of Missouri's largest springs, outside exhibits, picnic and shelter areas, and a playground. Other unique properties of the park include the Colosseum, which is believed to have formed naturally from caves collapsing and to have been used for Native American tribal meetings. Visit www.mostateparks.com for more information about Ha Ha Tonka.

LAKE OF THE OZARKS STATE PARK

If you have a water dog who loves to boat, then pick up an Aquatic Trail Map from the Lake of the Ozarks State Park. With stops between the main campground of the park at Public Beach #1 and Public Beach #2 (Grand Glaize Beach), this trail is just under ten miles. Each of the fourteen stops on the water trail is marked with an orange buoy. Enjoy boating on the lake while visiting the "Slice Arch" (a natural window in a bluff), the remains of lake reefs formed in ancient seas, and a naturally solar-heated bluff, among other interesting areas. With eleven paths, there is truly a trail for every type of hiker. Visitors can fish, camp, or even rent a boat at the park if they don't have their own. Visit www.mostateparks.com for additional information.

SIGHTS & EVENTS WORTH A LICK

BAGNELL DAM STRIP AND OVERLOOK

A trip to the town of Lake Ozark would not be complete without a stroll down the "Strip," where kitschy shops and tacky tourist attractions line both sides of the street. This area hasn't changed much over the decades—other than to expand. Be sure to grab a funnel cake and play some skee ball in the open-area arcade. After you've had your fill, drive northeast of the dam to the scenic overlook on Bagnell Dam Boulevard for an awesome view of Lake Ozark, the lake itself, the strip, and the Osage River. Here, visitors can learn about numerous historical facts of the area.

CANINE CANNONBALL

Paws down, Canine Cannonball is the **best canine activity** at the lake! Presented by Dock Dogs at Dog Days Bar & Grill, canines compete in three areas: the distance leap (the Big Air Wave), the vertical leap (referred to as the Extreme Vertical), and the timed retrieval race (the Speed Retrieve). This June event is free to watch and donations go to the no-kill Dogwood Animal Shelter of Camdenton, a most worthy cause. Live music, vendor displays, and pets from the shelter looking for forever homes accompany the competition. Whether your dog is competing or just observing, he'll have a barkin' good time. Dog Days Bar & Grill is located at 1232 Jeffries Road in Osage Beach and accessible by water at the 19-mile marker. To register your four-legged friend to compete or to learn more about this favorite event, go to www.dockdogs.com.

OMA & NOMA HERITAGE FESTIVAL

Honoring the first two individuals (Oma and Noma Deegraffenreid) to bravely cross Bagnell Dam after its construction was complete in 1931, this celebration features characters dressed in 1920–1940s attire, vintage automobiles and farming equipment, live Ozark blues and bluegrass music, storytellers, crafters, and other exhibits of that era. Enter the pie-eating, peanut-spitting, or bubble gum contests or the outhouse race. Better yet, get your dog dressed up in his period clothing and let him try his luck in the dog show or one of the **canine contests** where winners are awarded ribbons and prizes. Activities take place in May on and near Luby's Stage at 1359 Bagnell Dam Boulevard in Lake Ozark.

SEVEN SPRINGS WINERY

Although this winery hosts weddings and other events, the back patio or covered porch of this establishment is relaxing and ideal for you and Fido to just take in the magnificent view of the Ozark hills while you enjoy a glass of your favorite wine and something to eat. The menu offers appetizers, light fare options such as the seared Ahi tuna firecracker lollipops or their award-winning spicy shrimp and crab bisque, salads, paninis and wraps, burgers, flatbread, and dinner choices like the K.C. strip, in addition to a kids' menu. They've taken the guesswork out of it for those who aren't wine connoisseurs and have paired each menu item with a suggested wine. Seven Springs Winery is open daily from 11 a.m. to 7 p.m. and is located at 846 Winery Hills Estates in Linn Creek, between Osage Beach and Camdenton.

WHERE TO SIT & STAY

CAMDEN ON THE LAKE

For luxurious suites and everything you need right at the complex, you can't go wrong with Camden on the Lake. All suites are lakeview with fireplaces, kitchenettes, king beds with plush bedding, leather sofa sleepers, built-in flat screens and surround sound, as well as other quality details. An outdoor pool with swim-up bar, spa, beauty salon, restaurants, indoor sand volleyball court, and fitness center are all on-site. In addition, H. Toad's is next door with good food, cold drinks, and live entertainment. Located in Toad Cove, guests can dock their boats here as well. Located at 2359 Bittersweet Road in Lake Ozark, Camden on the Lake is just minutes from the **Bark Park.** Two dogs up to thirty-five pounds each are welcome for a $50 per night one-time fee.

CASA DE LOCO

Yes, it does mean House of Crazy, however, there's no need to be concerned. This winery/lodge was once an exclusive fishing destination and known as "The Millionaire's Club" due to the highfalutin St. Louisans that used to visit the property. Later, and after changing hands several times, the property became the Mozark Health Care Facility, which housed both the elderly and mentally ill patients, hence being referred to as Casa De Loco.

Just a short drive outside of Camdenton, the only thing loco about this place is the crazy beautiful view of the Niangua River from the bluff the lodge sits atop. Today, Casa De Loco Winery offers guests a beautiful place to fish, float the lake, and just get away from it all. Dogs can join their owners for a $15 fee, but are not allowed inside the winery. Go to www.casadelocowinery.com for a glimpse of the suites, the modern bath accommodations, and stellar views from this treasure nestled amongst the Ozark trees.

LODGE OF THE FOUR SEASONS

Celebrating fifty years in 2013, this waterfront resort is home to nationally recognized Spa Shiki, fifty-four holes of golf, an indoor and several outdoor pools, a fitness center, tennis courts, high-end shops, and even their own movie theater right on the property. Standard rooms with double beds as well as two Avila rooms that are located adjacent to the main lodge (one with two queens and the other with a king, kitchen, and living area) are available for travelers with pets. With several dining options on the property you can get an order to-go (including fine dining) or order room service to share with your pup. There is a $50 non-refundable pet fee per pet, and dogs must not weigh more than fifty pounds. Visit the **nearby Bark Park** or take Fido for a stroll on the walk path. Visit www.4seasonsresort.com to see all that this resort has to offer, including current packages available.

PROFESSIONAL MANAGEMENT GROUP, INC.

A reputable and longtime management company for local properties, PMG handles an abundance of rentals for homeowners and condominium complexes. Contacting them is a great option to take the legwork out of finding **pet-friendly properties,** which can be time consuming and frustrating (877-764-4253). Visitors can also contact the Convention & Visitors Bureau (573-348-1599) for a list of other agencies in the business of property management.

BEST BITES

ANDY'S FROZEN CUSTARD

For a frozen treat that is sure to satisfy both you and your pup (Andy's will serve up a scoop **just for Fido** upon request), visit 4820 Osage Beach Parkway. Not far from Lake of the Ozarks State Park, this is a great way to cool off after a long hike on one of the many trails. Choose from concretes, sundaes, malts, and more—all made with their secret blend of milk, cream, and sugar.

CREE MEE DRIVE-IN

Cree Mee in Eldon has been in business since 1952 and is still going strong, serving up their "World Famous" chili cheese dogs, marshmallow Pepsis, soft-serve ice cream, and other tasty treats. Walk up to the window or drive through, but definitely visit Cree Mee off Highway 54 at 801 S. Aurora.

DOG DAYS BAR & GRILL

With a name that honors man's best friend, the restaurant that hosts the **Canine Cannonball** (see page 74) will be your pup's favorite place at the lake. Lakefront with large deck and patio areas, Dog Days serves up some serious cuisine with everything from crab legs to baby back ribs. There's an extensive list of burgers and tacos to choose from as well as a menu just for puppies (kids). With live entertainment, great food, and a pet-friendly environment, the entire family will love Dog Days! Visit www.dogdays.com for a complete list of menu items and other events.

Photo courtesy Joyce Fulton

LI'L RIZZOS

Voted Best Italian Restaurant by *Lake Lifestyles Magazine* for three years in a row, Li'l Rizzos is the perfect place to order up a pizza to-go or have one delivered to you and your four-legged friend. In addition to great pies, they offer a full menu of Italian fare. Delivery is offered at the location in Osage Beach adjacent to the outlet mall at 929 Premium Outlets Drive (573-302-1500), but you'll have to carry out at the Lake Ozark site (573-365-3003), which is near both Camden on the Lake and the Lodge of the Four Seasons at 2196 Horseshoe Bend Parkway.

POSH PUPPY

FRIENDLY PAWS PET BOUTIQUE

For the hippest styles in **canine clothing,** cute gifts and collectibles, as well as unique dog and cat products, you'll want to visit Friendly Paws Pet Boutique at the Landing in Osage Beach. The boutique is open seven days a week for all your furry friend's shopping spree needs.

Photo courtesy Matt Hambly

LOVE DOGS, MUST TRAVEL: BEST OF MISSOURI

ST. LOUIS REGION

ST. CHARLES COUNTY

Home to the first State Capitol, Daniel Boone's home, annual festivals, and rich traditions, St. Charles County offers its canine visitors a sensational mix of entertainment, outdoor fun, and special experiences. A gem in the river town of St. Charles, Main Street has managed to maintain her Old World charm and offers those exploring this area a plethora of activities, as well as fine dining and boutique shopping. With several off-leash dog parks, miles of trails, historic sites, and unique places to stay, the fast-growing community of St. Charles County is inviting and affordable to its visitors.

PuppyPicks

R.T. Weiler's Food and Spirits

The décor at 201 N. Main Street is dog, dog, and more dog. With menu items like Y'appetizers, Bark BQ, and the build-your-own Mutt burger, your pup will think it's all about him. Remember to bring along a picture of your furry friend to add to the ones that already line the wall. The patio at R.T. Weiler's is a great place to sit and stay to enjoy Music on Main, but you'll need to get there early as tables fill up fast.

PARKS & TRAILS FOR TAILS

BROMMELSIEK

As one of the prettiest off-leash parks in the state, this fenced play area boasts log benches scattered about the gravel path, along with a lake where dogs can swim in warmer weather. Those that want to hone their skills can even practice jumping off the dock. With more than four miles of surrounding trail, even hard-to-wear-out dogs can get in a good hike before or after their park play. Unlike many others, this park has one fenced area for all sizes of dogs to socialize together. Brommelsiek is also host to Paws in the Park, an annual event featuring contests and prizes, along with K-9 demonstrations. **Dock Dogs** showed off their jumping skills in 2012 and were a huge hit. Wet conditions and inclement weather commonly cause the park to close, so it's a good idea to call the hotline (636-949-7475) prior to making the drive out to 1615 Schwede Road in Wentzville (www.sccmo.org/parks for a complete list of doggy etiquette).

LOVE DOGS, MUST TRAVEL: BEST OF MISSOURI

DUSABLE DOG PARK

Residents flock from all over the St. Louis area to this fee-free St. Charles dog park for some off-leash puppy play. The 2.5-acre park consists of three large rotating sections (one for large dogs, one for small, and one area set aside to allow the grass to grow back). It is rarely empty but large enough to never be overcrowded. There are benches, pavilions, picnic tables, and shade trees located throughout the park, which is open rain or shine. Restrooms and a water source are available in warmer months. In October, the St. Charles City Animal Control and the Frenchtown Association hold **Dogtoberfest,** an adoption event with games, contests, micro-chipping, and a parade that ends at DuSable Dog Park, which is conveniently adjacent to the Katy Trail. Canine-friendly vendors and organizations partake in this fun event with a cause. Visit www.stcharlesparks.com and www.saintcharlescitypets.com/dogtoberfest for more information.

FRONTIER PARK

Frontier Park, at 500 S. Riverside Drive along the Missouri River, is the hub for many St. Charles festivities throughout the year, such as **Trails for Tails,** and home to some unique sights. Visitors and locals alike fill the riverfront to shop for interesting craft items and sample local goodies (kettle corn made on-site is always a favorite) during popular events like the Festival of the Little Hills. Benches throughout the park make it a nice resting point for you and your pup to watch the flow of the river after walking or biking the Katy Trail that runs right through Frontier Park.

The Katy railroad depot resides in the park along with a lone Wabash railcar. Just south of the depot stands a fifteen-foot sculpture of Meriwether Lewis, William Clark, and Lewis's dog **Seaman,** in honor of their departure from and return to St. Charles from their westward expedition.

Fido Fact

Seaman set out from St. Charles in the spring of 1804 with the Corps of Discovery, which included his owner, Captain Meriwether Lewis, to explore westward land and people. Seaman was a Newfoundland, a breed known for their large size, strong swimming skills, and loyalty. According to entries in the journals of both Lewis and Clark, Seaman proved to be quite helpful on their journey by hunting for food and warding off the danger of wild animals such as grizzly bears and buffalo. On several occasions, the trip took such a toll on Seaman that Meriwether feared his death. Journal entries place him still with the Corps in 1806. It is unknown for certain whether Seaman returned to St. Charles with his master, as there is no documentation to prove it. Seaman is memorialized in St. Charles, in addition to numerous other places throughout the state of Missouri.

LOVE DOGS, MUST TRAVEL: BEST OF MISSOURI

KATY TRAIL

As the old route of the Missouri-Kansas-Texas rail line (also known as M-K-T and more commonly as the "Katy"), this trail stretches for 227 miles from the eastern town of Machens, across Missouri to Clinton on the western side of the state. A good amount of the trail follows the path of Lewis and Clark alongside the Missouri River. Many take in the natural beauty of the trail surroundings while biking or walking, although portions of the trail have more recently been approved for horseback riding. However, for those wanting to plan a more extensive Katy Trail trip, a complete list of towns that it runs through and the services offered there, along with mileage calculations, can be found at www.bikekatytrail.com. DuSable Dog Park is a convenient place to pick up the trail if you plan on visiting the park anyway. Heading south, this part of the trail leads to the boat ramp access off Second Street, and it then loops through a quiet and tranquil area amidst forest wildlife. Be sure to read the markers along the way, which provide historical insight and alert you to specific species native to that area of the trail.

SIGHTS & EVENTS WORTH A LICK

CHRISTMAS TRADITIONS

Christmas Traditions on Main Street is a cultural spectacle. White lights speckle the trees while characters of Christmas past share greetings and stories of the holidays. Horse-drawn carriages and shoppers loaded down with gifts line the cobblestone streets of this historic area, while strolling carolers entice you to sing along. There's the roasting of marshmallows and chestnuts, photo ops with Santa and the Clydesdales, parades, and even a kissing ball, in addition to the ceremonial lighting of the tree to kick off the season.

On the first Saturday night in December, the Las Posadas procession begins at the corner of Boone's Lick Road and South Main Street, honoring this longtime Spanish tradition mimicking Mary and Joseph's search for a room at the inn. The procession is lit with luminaries, candles, and lanterns and concludes with caroling, a live Nativity, and the Yule Log in Frontier Park. Bring your pup and join in the magical celebration of the season between Thanksgiving and Christmas.

FETE DE GLACE

For dogs that don't mind the cooler weather, the Festival of Ice on Main Street takes place in January, with competitors carving out large blocks of ice into dynamic creations. Grab a cup of hot chocolate, a sweater for your pup, and your ballots from the information booth that you'll find near the center of the festival. That's right! You and your furry friend, along with the other onlookers, get to judge the competition. Admission to this festival is free, with the carving starting in the morning and going until mid- to late afternoon. Look for the sculptures between the 100 and 200 blocks of Main Street in St. Charles near R.T. Weiler's.

LEWIS & CLARK BOAT HOUSE AND NATURE CENTER

The Lewis & Clark Boat House and Nature Center is located at 1050 Riverside at the river's edge. While pets are not allowed in the museum, there are numerous sites around the property to explore. The Boat House that sits on the lower level of the center houses the replicas of the boats used by **Seaman** and the other members of the Corps of Discovery. Notice the red and white pirogues, the keelboat, and dugout canoes. Outdoor markers along the walk paths and nature trail share information about events of the past and feature descriptions of native plants.

MUSIC ON MAIN

On the third Wednesday of the month from May to September, a cheerful crowd fills the street in front of restaurants R.T. Weiler's and Quintessential (referred to as Q by locals) for an evening of live music. Many bring lawn chairs to set up in the blocked-off street where local musicians play from 5:00 to 7:30. There's a beer tent where you can purchase a cold one, and a large portion of the crowd remains downtown to hit the bars and restaurants after the band finishes their performance.

OKTOBERFEST

On the last weekend of September, German dancers and singers provide some lively entertainment and everyone gathers in Frontier Park to hear the master yodeler. This action-packed weekend is one of the most festive and best events of the year in St. Charles. Experience some German heritage with a beer and a brat, line up to catch the Saturday morning parade, check out the car show, and by all means cheer on your favorite dachshund in the **Wiener Dog Race** and Fashion Show. This family-friendly event also features a children's area. Don't forget your lederhosen!

TRAILS FOR TAILS

Sponsored by Five Acres Animal Shelter, this annual event really gets the tails wagging. Your loyal companion will have a dog-gone good time working the **agility course,** participating in the walk or run, competing in Pace the Wind and other contests, and just hanging out with canine friends in Frontier Park. There are kiddie pools for lapping up water after the walk and treats to sample at the vendor tables. Furry friends in need of a loving home are at the event and on their very best behavior. Proceeds benefit Five Acres Animal Shelter, a no-kill facility.

VETERANS MEMORIAL

The St. Charles Veterans Memorial is located at the opposite end of Bishop's Landing and adjacent to Frontier Park. The War of 1812 was the first war in which St. Charles citizens participated with the U.S. Armed Forces. Thirty-five veterans of the war were laid to rest in cemeteries within St. Charles County. With a pavilion and black granite benches placed around the memorial, visitors can stop to reflect and pay tribute to those lost.

WHERE TO SIT & STAY

BOONE'S COLONIAL INN

As one of the four buildings that make up Stone Row on Historic Main Street in St. Charles, this boutique inn offers guests luxurious accommodations in a colonial setting. A gourmet breakfast for each night's stay is included, and you can request room service for an additional fee. Choose the Spanish or French Colonial Suite, or the most exquisite of the three offered—the Thomas Jefferson, which encompasses the entire second level. Be sure to let innkeepers know that you'll be bringing your dog (there's a reasonable fee of $35) and ask about any special packages available during the time of your visit. Go to www.boonescolonialinn.com for pictures of the elegant suites and to make reservations. No room at the inn? Inquire about pet-friendly rooms at Boone's Cottage and Boone's Lick Trail Inn located on South Main Street in St. Charles across from the Conservatory. Wouldn't Seaman be jealous if he could see your pup now?

DRURY INN

Located at 170 Mid Rivers Mall Circle adjacent to Mid Rivers Mall, this St. Peters hotel is extremely pet-friendly. All sizes of dogs are welcome and no fee is required. Amenities abound, including a complimentary hot breakfast and happy hour. This Drury has an indoor pool and whirlpool, a 24-hour fitness center, and offers two-room suites. For rates and special discounts visit www.druryhotels.com.

INNSBROOK

True dog lovers consider their pups family, and Innsbrook is the perfect escape for good old-fashioned family fun. Just west of St. Charles County, Innsbrook is a lake community with abundant activities and amenities. The following are excellent rentals available to your family, even the four-legged members. Innsbrook rules require pets to be on a leash at all times to protect this Audubon Sanctuary, and canines are not allowed on the beaches. Visit www.innsbrook-resort.com for policies and a list of the countless activities offered in this wildlife oasis.

1717 SONNENBLICK

Nestled amongst the forest, open fields, and lakes, the chalet at 1717 Sonnenblick is truly a home away from home. The 1,460 square-foot A-frame sleeps six and has two full baths, one on each level, in addition to large open family areas. Complete with cookware and utensils, the kitchen and full-size gas grill let you cook up a family meal without the pressures of home. The property has a large deck and boat dock. The kids will love the paddle boat, and the screened-in porch is a great place to relax any time of day. With a wall of windows overlooking the lake and a fireplace to cozy up to, this property is perfect in the colder months too. You and your dog can hike one of the many trails that wind through Innsbrook and visit the **off-leash dog park.** Bring a blanket and your furry friend and head over to the Farmhouse Field for live music and outdoor movie nights in the summer months. Up to two pets are allowed in the chalet for a one-time fee of $25 and there are no size limits or breed restrictions. To book the chalet you'll need to contact the owner. See: #201493 at www.vrbo.com and #207392 at www.homeaway.com.

1716 SONNENBLICK

This chalet sits directly across from 1717 Sonnenblick and makes a perfect addition if you have a large party. The property looks like a chalet on the outside but is luxurious with beautiful furnishings and modern interior décor. 1716 has a home theater system, oversized jet tub, fireplace, and sleeps two to four. To reserve and view gorgeous pictures of this spa-like property, go to www.homeaway.com, rental #903292 or www.vrbo.com, #323351.

BEST BITES

BRADDENS

With umbrellas for shade, fire pits for brisk days, a waterfall, and a pond, Braddens has one of the most inviting patios in St. Charles. Large enough to accommodate up to one hundred guests, there's plenty of room to bring along man's best friend for their much-loved weekend brunch. The Sunday chicken dinner is quite popular as well and includes enough chicken, mashed potatoes with gravy, corn on the cob, salad, and biscuits for two. Save room for homemade dessert. Braddens is open seven days a week and sits at 515 S. Main Street in St. Charles.

LLYWELYN'S PUB

Pubs came about as a place for travelers to rest and have a drink, and the patio with a river view at Llywelyn's is perfect for just that. There's rarely a visit to this establishment without a sighting of another four-legged friend, so your pooch will feel right at home. Located in an old bank building at 100 N. Main Street, this pub serves up Celtic fare in a lively atmosphere. Whether you visit for lunch, dinner, or just to take a midday break, you'll want to order up a basket of their Welsh potato chips for starters. Other locations include Central West End, Soulard, Webster Groves, and Winghaven.

OLD MILLSTREAM INN RESTAURANT AND BEER GARDEN

Old Millstream provides outdoor seating on one of their many patio areas in a serene setting with sun, shade, and fire pits. While many just come here to have a cold one with their pup in tow, the menu also offers guests some really tasty options for lunch and dinner. With over one hundred different bottled and canned beers in stock daily, you're sure to find one that satisfies. Old Mill is located at 912 S. Main Street next to Trailhead Brewery.

PICASSO'S COFFEE HOUSE

With tables available on the sidewalk year-round and a **dog bowl** of water just outside the front door, you'll see all types here, including canine. Make this your first stop of the day for a morning specialty coffee and fresh bakery item before you explore the riverfront with your dog. Or stop in for lunch after shopping on Main Street. Popular for open mic nights, Picasso's also serves liqueurs, beer, and wine. Be sure to order one of Pablo's real fruit smoothies to share with your loyal companion (www.picassoscoffeehouse.com).

THE VINE WINE BAR & BISTRO

The Vine is just across the cobblestone street from Boone's Colonial Inn. Once you settle into your room, head on over to the front courtyard for an exquisite dinner complemented by soothing music, fine wine, and your **loyal companion at your feet.** Fire pits offer a bit of warmth on cooler nights and add to the ambiance of this laid-back fine-dining experience. The lobster bisque is a menu fave and with fares like the filet with Parmesan and portabella and chestnut mushrooms, you can't go wrong. One of my personal favorites is the pecan-almond-crusted salmon with saffron risotto. The Vine is open nightly for dinner, with additional hours for special parties, and offers a unique and charming dining experience in the heart of downtown St. Charles.

POSH PUPPY

CANINE COOKIES N CREAM DOG BAKERY

Sure to be your four-legged friend's favorite stop in St. Charles, this bakery has gone completely to the dogs! Offering artistically decorated delectable treats made with all-natural ingredients fit for even human consumption, your pooch won't be able to choose just one. Cards fans will definitely want one of the Cardinal Squirrels, and the peanut butter–flavored frozen yogurt is always a hit with Kaia and Harlie. Let your loyal companion sniff out some sweet treats, new toys, or a cute gift for a canine friend back home. At 822 S. Main Street, Canine Cookies N Cream Dog Bakery is nestled in Historic St. Charles just up from the riverfront.

JAKE'S ON MAIN

Life is good when you're a dog and shopping at Jake's on Main! The Life Is Good line inspires people to do what they like and like what they do. Fido will definitely like what he's doing when he's nosing through the **Good Dog Gear** for a new toy, collar, bowl, or other clever item featuring Rocket (Jake's canine friend). Jake's on Main is located at 136 S. Main Street and hosts the Life Is Good Festival each year in St. Charles.

TREATS UNLEASHED

Treats Unleashed is across from Mid Rivers Mall and just down the way from the Drury Inn St. Peters. With treats made and baked on-site, your pup won't be able to resist a lick before leaving the store. Fun toys, along with collars, food, and other pet products line the shelves where the staff is always so friendly and helpful. Self-wash stations and **full-service grooming** are also available. Visit their website for events currently taking place in the stores throughout the St. Louis area, www.treats-unleashed.com.

THE YUPPY PUPPY PET SPA

With over ten years under its paws, the Yuppy Puppy certainly knows how to **pamper your pet.** Visit the Yuppy Puppy Pet Spa in O'Fallon for a canine mani/pedi with nail painting, aromatherapy, blueberry-vanilla facial, or have some earrings put on. Yuppy Puppy also offers pet sitting, boarding, playcamp, and typical grooming services. Call 636-625-0030 to schedule an appointment. Yuppy Puppy is located at 3018 Winghaven Boulevard in O'Fallon.

ST. LOUIS

As one of the most dog-friendly cities in the state of Missouri, St. Louis has a wealth of outdoor adventures for pooches. There are numerous canine events honoring our furry friends, an abundance of trails and parks where Fido can run and play, and a plethora of restaurants where your loyal companion can accompany you as you dine. Forest Park (home to the 1904 World's Fair) is an outdoor playground, while the resurgence of the downtown area now offers guests of the city the most modern cuisine and accommodations. St. Louis consists of many distinct communities, each offering its own flavor of entertainment. With areas like the Loop, Soulard, and Central West End (just to name a few), visitors will never run out of things to do. While well-known for non-canine features such as the Arch and the Saint Louis Zoo, the Gateway City also offers countless hidden gems (many of which are free) for you and your furry friend to find. "See Red" with your pup at a Cardinals baseball game or let him prance his paws at the Mardi Gras parade, but be sure to allow plenty of time to explore the great city of St. Louis.

PARKS & TRAILS FOR TAILS

CASTLEWOOD STATE PARK

This 1,818-acre state park in southwest St. Louis County has eight hiking trails of varying length for you and your dog. The Meramec River runs through the park and offers spectacular views along the hike.

FOREST PARK

Forest Park is one of the largest urban parks in the country, and with over 12 million visitors a year, it is constantly bustling with activity. Home to the famous Saint Louis Zoo, St. Louis Art Museum, Missouri History Museum, the Muny Opera House, Saint Louis Science Center, and green space complemented by bike and jogging paths, there's something to do here for all types, including our furry friends. The Forest Park Balloon Race and countless other events take place at the park annually. Forest Park even hosted the World's Fair in 1904. Sled down Art Hill, visit the outdoor exhibits, or take a brisk walk through the park situated within the heart of St. Louis. Afterwards, grab some lunch at the Boathouse where you're sure to see other canines dining.

JEFFERSON BARRACKS PARK

Named in honor of President Thomas Jefferson on land he obtained through the Louisiana Purchase, Jefferson Barracks was a significant military post. On the Mississippi River and near the hub of St. Louis, the site was critical in every war in the United States until it was deactivated in 1946. Non-aggressive pooches are welcome on the property everywhere except in the buildings and at the informational area for visitors. Original barracks and stone buildings from the post still remain. There's a scenic overlook high above the Mississippi River along the trail with covered shelters where you can lunch. Today, Jefferson Barracks remains rich with history and hosts current special events throughout the year, including weddings and historical re-enactments. Jefferson Barracks consists of 426 acres and is located at 345 N. Road in St. Louis.

PAW PARK

Paw Park is a one-acre off-leash park located at Bradley Beach Road and Jeffco Boulevard in Arnold. The park is open from sunrise to sunset and is free to use. The fenced park is divided with a side for dogs twenty-four pounds and under and a separate side for larger dogs. The Watchdog Program (volunteers monitoring dogs and their companions to be sure rules are being followed) makes this off-leash area safer and more enjoyable for all visitors.

Dog Parks

St. Louis City and County are littered with dog parks, but the majority are not open to the public, which is a major reason why DuSable Dog Park in nearby St. Charles County is popular throughout the region.

ST. LOUIS REGION

QUAIL RIDGE DOG PARK

Quail Ridge Dog Park is 1.5 acres and offers separate sides for small and big pooches, benches, and shade. It is open from dawn to dusk and is surrounded by trails where you and Fido can take a nice hike or walk before or after play with other pups. It is located within Quail Ridge Park (250 acres) in Wentzville where visitors can fish, play disc golf or horseshoes, and picnic, among other outdoor activities. Fetching, chasing, and frolicking are all free at this park!

QUEENY PARK

This St. Louis County park offers you and your pup five different trails to hike—with the longest being the Hawk Ridge Trail at 4.4 miles. Together, the Dogwood, Fox Run, Hawk Ridge, Owl Creek, and White Oak trails equal over seven miles. In addition to a playground and tennis courts, there are numerous stocked lakes at Queeny Park where you and your pooch can fish. The website (www.stlouisco.com) provides park information including a detailed map of the trails and which plants and animals to avoid while hiking this hilly area. (Venomous snakes are rarely encountered; however, there are two species possibly living within the park.) Queeny Park is also home to the Dog Museum, a St. Louis attraction your four-legged friend will want to visit (see facing page).

SIGHTS & EVENTS WORTH A LICK

AMERICAN KENNEL CLUB MUSEUM OF THE DOG

In Queeny Park, the Museum of the Dog gets Top Dog billing, with all things dedicated to man's best friend. The 14,000-square-foot facility houses more than seven hundred pieces of artwork, all of which depict the dog. It can be rented out for events, including those for dogs. On Saturdays and Sundays the **Guest Dog** of the Week is invited to meet museum visitors. Call 314-821-3647 for a current schedule. The museum is closed on some holidays and in extreme weather conditions in order to conserve energy.

"Great Dane" oil on canvas by the English artist Maud Earl, courtesy Museum of the Dog

ST. LOUIS REGION

APA'S CANINE CARNIVAL

The annual Canine Carnival is the major fund-raiser for the Animal Protective Association of Missouri. A **Canine King and Queen** are crowned each year in this longstanding event. Even if your dog doesn't reach a noble status, there are plenty of games, contests, and treats to keep him happy. The carnival includes a Pooch Parade and is held at St. Louis County's Tilles Park. Please visit the APA's website for additional information at www.apamo.org.

BARK IN THE PARK

This annual event is held in May in Forest Park. It's not only tons of fun for your furry friend, but it also supports the homeless at the Humane Society of Missouri. The morning starts off with a pancake breakfast, followed by a 5K run and walk, and then rolls right into **Incredible Dog Performances.** They have contests, a silent auction, and lots of excitement and playtime for Fido. Go to www.hsmo.org to register and view a list of events and times.

CITY GARDEN

The City Garden is at 801 Market Street, just down from the Hilton St. Louis Ballpark and Busch Stadium. Featuring twenty-four unique sculptures by an array of artists, the works are displayed amidst fountains and wading pools for children, in addition to carefully chosen landscaping. Maps of the garden can be printed at www.citygardenstl.org, and self-guided audio tours with use of your smart phone or a borrowed mp3 player offer insight into each piece. Joe's Chili Bowl, located within the garden, offers an extensive menu for breakfast, lunch, and dinner. Grab some take-out and enjoy a picnic in City Garden, where the culture is rich and admission is free. Baggies for your doggie's waste are available in the park, but pups are not allowed in the pools.

DISC DOGS

St. Louis Disc Dogs is a group of **frisbee pups** that perform routines and demonstrate their skills around the St. Louis area for entertainment. The have performed at the Mardi Gras Pet Parade, Bark in the Park, at Purina Farms, and numerous other popular events. For current events, visit www.discdogevents.com.

DOG DAYS CELEBRATION

Your pup will surely want to visit the Kirkwood Farmers' Market in September for the Dog Days Celebration. With special appearances by animal welfare groups, pet products for sale, and a pet parade this event has certainly **gone to the dogs!** See www.downtownkirkwood.com for details.

DOG SWIM–KIRKWOOD

Let your furry friend swim with the big dogs, and little ones too. The Missouri Alliance for Animal Legislation along with Pool Paws for Humane Laws sponsors **canine pool parties** at the Kirkwood Aquatic Center. The cost is $10 per dog/companion, with an additional $3 fee for additional people. Current immunization records are required. A portion of the proceeds goes toward the lobbying of animal welfare issues. Visit www.maal.org for more information about this event.

No Bones About It

Designed by Eero Saarinen, the St. Louis Arch is a 630-foot sight to behold and is the tallest monument in the United States. Representing the Westward Expansion, it is a must-see while visiting St. Louis and is so tall that visitors can admire its beauty from places all over the city, including Busch Stadium. From the top of the Arch you can take in stunning views, though your pup won't be able to make the trip up with you. Instead, take in the awesome view from the ground below or book a hotel room with an Arch view where Fido can join you.

LAUMEIER SCULPTURE PARK

Pack up your pooch and head out to Laumeier for some art in the park. As a free year-round outdoor activity, Laumeier Sculpture Park is an ideal way for you and your pup to get some exercise while admiring unique artwork. Visitors can check out an iPod from the museum or use their smart phones in conjunction with the sight/sound feature. Composer Eric Hall reached out to local artists and musicians to create an aural portrait of one of the permanent sculptures within the park as a reaction to, in conversation with, or as an extension of the work through the medium of sound. While there is no charge, a valid credit card must be left in exchange while the iPod is in use. A site map for the outdoor galleries is posted on the website, and you should check for scheduled special events, when dogs are not permitted in the park. Dogs must be up to date on vaccinations and leashed at all times while in the park, which is located at 12580 Rott Road in St. Louis.

LOOP ICE CARNIVAL

Already dressed in his coat, your pup will love this annual January event in the Loop where you can watch human dogsled races, hear live music, roast marshmallows, admire the ice sculptures, or participate in the **Frozen Buns Run.** There are jugglers, carnival rides, ice slides, and ice smashing (real money is inside) too!

POOCHES IN THE BALLPARK

The Cardinals welcome their **furry fans** to one game each year at Busch Stadium. The date changes yearly, and the event is popular, so be vigilant and plan very far ahead. It is much easier to google the event than to attempt to navigate the Cardinals' website. Dogs and their owners get their own section in the stadium, and the ticket gets owners all-you-can-eat food and drink.

Fido Fact

Quentin, a cute Basenji mix, was known as Cain and was a starving puppy when his owner gave him up and signed off on his execution papers. In the early 2000s, dogs met their unfortunate fate in the gas chamber. Defying all odds, he somehow survived the chamber, and from that day on his life changed for the better. He was the only dog in the country ever known to have survived gas chamber euthanasia and the St. Louis center that had him could only think of one thing to do. They called Randy Grim, who was well known for his work with strays and is founder of Stray Rescue of St. Louis, a no-kill facility. Today, Quentin and Randy are friends and partners in the fight for animal welfare. For ways that you can help or to learn more about Quentin the Miracle Dog, go to www.strayrescue.org.

ST. LOUIS WALK OF FAME

Approximately 250 brass stars and bronze plaques make up the St. Louis Walk of Fame on Delmar Boulevard. Honorees must have either been born in or have spent their creative years in St. Louis. Honorees include Ozzie Smith, Maya Angelou, Robert Duvall, Chuck Berry, Yogi Berra, T. S. Eliot, Lou Brock, Tina Turner, Charles Lindbergh, and Jackie Joyner-Kersee—several of whom still live in and around the St. Louis area. Let your pup sniff out his favorite stars as you walk, shop, and eat your way down Delmar in the Loop.

PuppyPicks

Purina Farms

Purina is dedicated to making the lives of our pets better. The company allows pooches to come to work with their owners each day. Purina Farms is home to numerous canine events and competitions, many of which are free to spectators and their dogs. If your furry friend enjoys listening to music, shopping, eating, and summertime, then she'll love Pet-A-Palooza, which is dedicated to adoption awareness. Once she gets her pic snapped in the photo booth and masters the agility course, she can lead the kids over to the children's area. In the fall, Purina Farms welcomes you and your loyal companion to watch furry friends show off their amazing talents in the Incredible Pet Challenge. If your pup has a competitive nature or special talent, you can sign her up for the Canine Games, Disc Flying, Talent Contest, or one of the many other competitions held at Purina Farms Event Center. Because the event facility is rented out to sponsors of other canine organizations, you'll need to confirm that your dog is allowed to come along for each individual event. For a list of all the family-friendly activities at Purina Farms, a calendar of events, pictures, bios of the resident pets, and directions to the facility in Gray Summit, visit www.purinafarms.com.

STRUT YOUR MUTT

Join your loyal companion in a leisurely walk to raise money for homeless animals. After the walk, treat your pup to a massage, paw reading, and **free treats** while partaking in all the other festival activities. This event takes place in September in Queeny Park.

SOULARD MARDI GRAS

The Mardi Gras celebration in St. Louis is quite the event, lasting for several weeks. Soulard, one of the oldest communities within St. Louis City, hosts one of the largest carnivals in the country with visitors traveling many, many miles to take part in the fun. There are pub crawls, family festivities, musical performances, tons of food options, the Wiener Dog Derby, and of course parades, including a **pet parade.** The Beggin' Barkus Pet Parade is one of the largest animal parades in the world. It gives your mutt a chance to strut his stuff and meet lots of new canine friends. Go to www.mardigrasinc.com for the event lineup.

©RiverCityImages 2013

TASTE OF ST. LOUIS

Taste of St. Louis appeals to all types and provides unique and exciting experiences for its participants. More than 400,000 people attended in September of 2012. This downtown event at Twelfth and Market streets near Soldiers' Memorial celebrates the best of St. Louis with a mix of art, food, music, and culture. Sample wine on the Art & Wine Walk, explore the many booths in the Marketplace, and take in the talent at Center Stage. Of course, the best part is taste-testing the culinary skills of St. Louis's finest foodies.

WHERE TO SIT & STAY

THE CHESHIRE INN

With a **Noble Pet Program** and a director of Pet Relations on staff, this St. Louis boutique hotel will treat your pup like royalty from the moment she arrives. There's a special VIP treat at check-in, and pet amenities such as a doggie bed, two-section bowl, and other goodies from Nestle Purina are in the room. With all the canine amenities, amazingly, there is no pet fee. However, dogs are limited to sixty pounds. Arrangements for doggie massage, walkers and sitters, and other special services can be made upon request. Employees at the Fox & Hounds tavern, located on the property, can even pack a picnic lunch for you and your four-legged friend to take to nearby Forest Park. The Cheshire Inn provides loaner leashes, maps of local dog parks and runs, as well as a pet-friendly outdoor area. Fido is allowed in any room, including the novelty suites (James Bond, Romeo and Juliet, and Passage to India). Be sure to pre-register your dog so the Cheshire can prepare for her arrival.

DRURY INN AT UNION STATION AND UNION MARKET

As noted in other sections in this book, the Drury Inn is consistently the most pet-friendly hotel chain in Missouri. The historic Union Station and Union Market locations are no exception. Union Market is across the street from the Edward Jones Dome. See page 35 for a description of what Drury Inn has to offer.

FOUR SEASONS HOTEL

With no pet fee and its sophisticated, modern décor, this luxury AAA Five Diamond hotel is pawsitively pooch perfect and mere blocks from the St. Louis riverfront. Plenty of types of rooms are available, but be sure to request one with a city view so you can gaze at the Arch through your floor-to-ceiling windows. Offering its guests plush bedding, nightly turn-down service, thick bathrobes and slippers upon request, along with L'Occitane bath amenities, your pup might just want to stay in and order a four-course meal from Cielo. Nominated as the Best Open Air Hang Out and Best Restaurant in St. Louis, Cielo dishes up savory signature dishes sure to satisfy even the hardest-to-please palate. Dogs are not allowed on the terrace patio or in the casino and are limited to two per room, with neither dog to exceed fifty pounds.

THE HILTON ST. LOUIS AT THE BALLPARK

Just steps from the St. Louis Arch and Busch Stadium, this hotel provides rooms with magnificent views of the infield or the Arch. With numerous restaurants on the property, including a Starbucks and Yo My Goodness (I bet your pooch is drooling right now), you won't even need to leave the hotel to curb your hunger. New and trendy rooftop bar and restaurant 360 offers stunning views of the city and mouthwatering concoctions from truffled popcorn to steak and seafood, while Mike Shannon's Steak and Seafood (owned by St. Louis Cardinals sportscaster and former player) sits adjacent to the Hilton. There is a gift shop, pool, and fitness center, as well as children's activities available for guest use. A $75 nonrefundable one-time fee covers multiple pets up to seventy-five pounds, and all dogs must be kenneled if left unattended in the room. Fido can run the bases in his sleep while snuggled in tight high above Busch Stadium.

MILLENNIUM HOTEL

The Millennium Hotel in downtown St. Louis, like the Hilton, is positioned between Busch Stadium and the Gateway Arch. Dogs are allowed in standard rooms in the south tower only, but there is no pet fee, no dog limit, and no weight limit. Unfortunately, Fido is not welcome at the Top of the Riverfront, which is a revolving restaurant on the twenty-eighth floor.

MOONRISE HOTEL

As one of the region's leading green hotels, this sophisticated and chic boutique hotel resides in the heart of the Loop. Named for the streetcars that once "looped around" for their return to St. Louis, the Delmar Loop is a vibrant neighborhood complete with unique shopping, diverse entertainment, and popular restaurants. Amenities abound in all rooms. Ten "Walk of Fame" suites are available; each is named and themed after one of the stars featured on the St. Louis Walk of Fame on Delmar. Let your pet stretch his paws out with the "Bewitched" Agnes Moorehead, or howl it out with "King of Horror" Vincent Price. One thing is sure: He won't feel like Jed Clampett from *The Beverly Hillbillies* in the contemporary Buddy Ebsen Suite. Because **pets are family** too, beds as well as food and water bowls are provided for your dog or cat upon check-in. All dog sizes are allowed for a one-time $50 fee. With 24-hour room service, you won't have to leave your pet behind to indulge in a meal from the award-winning Eclipse on-site restaurant. Although your pup isn't allowed to join you, you'll want to visit the Rooftop Terrace Bar for a drink and the most amazing view! Be sure to check out the website for special packages and rates (www.moonrisehotel.com). For above and beyond service, simply contact the Manager of Desires, who can arrange for birthday balloons, flowers, and other special accommodations to send your stay over the top.

BEST BITES

BEVO MILL

The location of 4749 Gravois was chosen by August A. Busch Sr. due to its proximity between his home at Grant's Farm and the Anheuser-Busch Brewery. He set out to build an authentic Dutch mill and used the Mill Room for his own private dining area, while the rest of the restaurant was open to the public. Now open for special events and one of the best brunches around, Bevo Mill welcomes canine friends on the patio and provides treats and water with one look of those puppy-dog eyes. For more Bevo Mill history and the Sunday Brunch menu, go to www.thebevomill.com.

PI PIZZERIA

Just across the street from Moonrise Hotel, you'll find the best pizza around. Order up the freshest of ingredients on your favorite crust (even vegan and gluten-free are available upon request) and save room for the apple pi for dessert. Your dog is welcome at a sidewalk table, where you both can watch passersby. Pi is open for breakfast too, with an assortment of fresh-baked goods, waffles, and a breakfast pizza. For a complete list of menu items, go to www.restaurantpi.com.

LLYWELYN'S PUB

A destination neighborhood in St. Louis, Soulard is the place to be. You and Fido can enjoy the local culture while dining at a sidewalk table at Llywelyn's. Grab a beer and order up some Celtic food to enjoy while you watch the action. In addition to the Soulard location, guests can visit Llywelyn's in the Central West End, Webster Groves, Wildwood, St. Charles, or Winghaven.

THE BOATHOUSE

As one of the most popular canine-friendly restaurants in St. Louis, the Boathouse offers more than just boating. Nestled in Forest Park at the edge of Post-Dispatch Lake, this favorite eatery allows dogs to join their human companions outdoors for lunch, dinner, or just a drink by the lake. Sunday brunch is served from 10:00 a.m. to 3:00 p.m. Weather permitting, paddleboats and one- or two-person kayaks are available to rent, with a Moonlight Paddleboat Picnic on Thursday evenings. Dogs are welcome on the boats. Friday evenings bring live musical guests in the beer garden and special events take place throughout the year. Visit the Boathouse in Forest Park and let Fido do the **dog paddling** (www.boathouseforestpark.com).

Photo courtesy Lynn Terry Photography and www.lynnterry.com

LOVE DOGS, MUST TRAVEL: BEST OF MISSOURI

RUE LAFAYETTE CAFÉ

After a walk by the ponds and across the bridge in Lafayette Park, cross the street to French-inspired Rue Lafayette. Weather permitting, the band will be singing and swinging outside on the front patio where you can order up some delicious brunch. Sip on a Bella-ini (inspired by Bella the Boston terrier, whom you may see wearing pink stylish goggles coming or going while riding in the owner's convertible) and take in the 1920s architecture of Rue's refurbished building and the historic neighborhood that surrounds this café. Rue Lafayette proudly offers light-as-a-feather croissants and melt-in-your-mouth macaroons along with other pastries, wines, beer, and a full espresso bar. Rue Lafayette is open for breakfast and lunch, hosts local book signings as well as other events, and donates to local organizations that support animals in need.

SQUARE ONE BREWERY & DISTILLERY

A great place for good food and cold drinks, Square One is also dog-friendly. Bring your loyal companion along with you for lunch, dinner, or to indulge in the tasty Sunday brunch. Square One Brewery is located at 1727 Park Avenue.

SQWIRES RESTAURANT

SqWires offers the finest steaks and seafood along with more casual fare. On Thursdays between Memorial Day and Labor Day, you and Fido can stop by for barbeque on the patio or take it to-go. In the heart of the Lafayette Square historic district, SqWires is located at 1415 S. 18th Street and is open Tuesday–Saturday.

TED DREWES FROZEN CUSTARD

To some St. Louis natives, Ted Drewes Frozen Custard has become a staple in their diets. In business since 1929, Ted Drewes has become nationally known for their creamy frozen custard concoctions. Try the Root 66 flavor or order a Crater Copernicus or Terra Mizzou off the specialty menu. Ted Drewes also sells Christmas trees, hand-picked by Ted from Nova Scotia each holiday season. Stop by 6726 Chippewa or the one on South Grand to lap up an old-time cold treat.

WILD FLOWER

Situated in the hip Central West End at the corner of Laclede and Euclid, this eatery provides a casual, relaxing atmosphere with great food. With such an extensive menu, it won't be easy to decide, but the truffled mac 'n cheese and sea bass are both out of this world good! This restaurant with a heart sponsors their annual **Party for Pets** in the fall and gives a generous 25 percent of the proceeds to Stray Rescue of St. Louis. Visit for brunch, lunch, or dinner seven days a week.

POSH PUPPY

FOUR MUDDY PAWS

Four Muddy Paws at 1711 Park Avenue in Lafayette Square offers their guests great products, a large self-grooming dog wash area, grooming service, and lots of free helpful information. Better yet, they host Yappy Hour Wine Tastings and **Dining Out with Your Dog** nights, which start at Four Muddy Paws for wine tasting and patio play time, then move on to pet-friendly local restaurants like SqWires and Square One Brewery. As host to professionals in the pet field and numerous events, this is the perfect place to come see Santa, get some connective canine bodywork, or engage in an animal communication session. This is a favorite source for finding current fur-friendly activities (www.fourmuddypaws.com).

LOLA & PENELOPE'S PREMIERE PET BOUTIQUE

For high-end fashion and the coolest pet products, head over to Lola & Penelope's at 7742 Forsyth Boulevard in Clayton. With name-brand products like Juicy Couture, Sniffany & Co., and **Chewy Vuitton,** your pup will think she died and went to heaven. As to not leave out the guardians, there are cute designs from House of Barkology and Life Is Good for canine moms, and even pet-themed jewelry. Running short on time? Visit and order online at www.lolaandpenelopes.com.

ST. LOUIS REGION

KENNELWOOD PET RESORT

If you must separate from Fido while traveling the St. Louis area, then Kennelwood at Page & Lindbergh is the place for her. She can romp and play at **daycamp** with furry friends and even retire to a private villa where she can watch Animal Planet and receive personalized care. Your pup will be treated as a human or better here and even the strangest owner requests are taken seriously. Kennelwood has seven locations in the St. Louis region and also offers grooming, training, and pet products. Visit www.kennelwood.com to view accommodations of each location.

Photo courtesy Kennelwood Pet Resort

PETS IN THE CITY

Pets in the City, located in Historic Soulard on Twelfth Street, stocks organic and holistic products such as all-natural food, supplements, and, of course, treats! They have lots of great supplies and offer training classes and grooming services too. A great feature of Pets in the City is the self-wash station, which has two tub sizes to save human backs and provides bathers with several shampoos and conditioners at no extra charge. Towels and a dryer for less timid dogs are also available. Don't forget to acknowledge Kramer, the resident cat and the obvious one in charge, before heading next door to Nadine's Gin Joint for some breakfast, lunch, or dinner on the patio (www.thecitypet.com and www.nadinesginjoint.com).

TREATS UNLEASHED

For fresh-baked treats, grooming, and toys that provide man's best friend with hours of fun, visit Treats Unleashed. Fido will love shopping for all his needs here where the staff is exceptionally helpful! With five stores in the St. Louis region alone, there's sure to be one nearby (www.treats-unleashed.com).

TRUE VISION ONE

Thomas True, owner and photographer at True Vision One, must have some magical power over pups! With a simple squeak of a toy and some odd mouth noises he gets them to sit, stay, and even smile in just a matter of minutes. He snaps away and in no time produces reasonably priced **puppy pics.** Give him a call and get your pup shot at one of the many great places he travels to within the Show-Me State (314-537-7612/www.truevisionone.com).

WOLFGANG'S PET SHOP

Wolfgang's is located in the fashionable Central West End at 330 N. Euclid Avenue. The shop offers grooming and **doggie daycare,** along with birthday and "bark-mitzvah" parties for your four-legged friends. See pictures and more at www.wolfgangspetshop.com.

ST. LOUIS REGION

WHINE TRAIL

Nearly four decades after Prohibition, Missouri wineries regained their foothold. Today, more than one hundred wineries populate Missouri. Grape harvesting is not only a booming industry, but many Missourians enjoy visiting vineyards and wineries with man's best friend.

Settled among little river towns and amidst the Midwest's rolling hills, the drive to Missouri wine country is calming and the views are breathtaking. Most wineries offer snacks of cheeses, sausages, and crackers, and some serve full meals. A handful even offer gourmet dining. There's no shortage of national and even international awards going to winemakers of Missouri. Whether you prefer Vignoles, Norton (Missouri's official grape), Seyval, or another type of grape, there's a wine waiting for you along with a gorgeous view at one of Missouri's favorite canine-friendly wineries. Many bottles can even be purchased online or in your local grocery store.

PuppyPicks

Serious wine lovers should download the Missouri Wines app from iTunes or www.missouriwine.org.

LOVE DOGS, MUST TRAVEL: BEST OF MISSOURI

WINERIES WORTH A SIP

CHANDLER HILL VINEYARDS

Full-service winery Chandler Hill Vineyards sits atop a hill overlooking Femme Osage Valley, which once held the small cabin of freed slave Joseph Chandler. There is plenty of room for your four-legged friends on the 4,500-square-foot deck, which provides guests with comfortable lounge seating as well as tables. Live music entertains visitors, and there's more to munch on than cheese and crackers. The restaurant serves up shared plates, soups, salads, and sandwiches to nibble on while you sip away. To enjoy one of the many Missouri or California varieties offered here along with a breathtaking view of the vineyards, visit Chandler Hill at 596 Defiance Road in Defiance.

LA DOLCE VITA WINERY

With an extensive list of sandwiches, pizzettes, quiche, salads, and appetizers, there's no shortage of yummy items to go with your choice of wine. The owners of this winery pride themselves on welcoming guests to a relaxing atmosphere with beautiful views, live entertainment, and La Dolce Vita (the sweet life). This establishment can be found at 4 Lafayette Street in Washington.

MOUNT PLEASANT ESTATES

Established in 1859, Mount Pleasant is the oldest winery in Augusta and has a large patio and grassy areas on which their guests can linger. Mount Pleasant has a healthy wine selection and offers freshly ordered wraps, burgers, sandwiches, and salads from their Appellation Café as well as gourmet grab-n-go items. Mount Pleasant is an award winner for sustainable farming procedures. Located at 5634 High Street, this winery is open year-round but does have seasonal hours. Check the website for detailed information about their sustainable farming practices, the heritage of the winery, and specific hours (www.mountpleasant.com).

WINE COUNTRY GARDENS

Wine Country Gardens, a forty-two-acre nursery and farm that sits above the majestic Missouri River Valley, is just ten minutes south of Highway 40 at 2711 Defiance Road. With three large patios and lush grounds, you and your pup can pick the perfect spot to have lunch any day of the week or listen to music on a Sunday afternoon. Menu items include appetizers, hot sandwiches, soups, salads, and desserts. Grab a glass of wine and stroll through the rows of flowers, leisurely watch the swans on the pond, and let the sound of the waterfalls soothe all your cares away—all with Fido in tow. With breathtaking views and lovely landscaping, Wine Country Gardens was featured in *Better Homes and Gardens*. The venue holds many events year-round, so be sure to check the website for current information (www.winecountrygardens.net).

YELLOW FARMHOUSE VINEYARD

A country farmhouse, now known as Yellow Farmhouse Vineyard, occupies the rolling hills at 100 Defiance Road. The Farmhouse is a perfect way to lounge away a weekend day: there's live music, a scenic picnic area, and a wine garden. However, the best spot in the house is the big and grassy Picnic Hill, which is scattered with brightly colored chairs for guests to breathe in the view while savoring one of the flavorful wines. The wine flows and so do the **dog biscuits.** Be sure to have your pup ask for one. Grab a picnic lunch and have your loyal companion sniff out the perfect spot on the hill for a lovely time at Yellow Farmhouse Vineyard. For the history of how Yellow Farmhouse came to be, a list of their wines, along with their hours, go to www.yellowfarmhousewines.com.

WHERE TO SIT & STAY

PARSON'S HOUSE B&B

Built in 1842, the Federal-style Parson's House is considered the gateway to the Missouri River Wine Country and has a great view of the river and offers complimentary limo service. This B&B welcomes preapproved, well-behaved pups and is close to the Katy Trail in Defiance, making it a great option for Fido. After a day of tastings you can relax in Phoebe's Suite or a room with your own fireplace. Go to www.parsonshousebandb.com.

SUPER 8

The Super 8 Washington is located at 2081 Eckelkamp Court just off exit 251 of I-44. A free hot continental breakfast is offered along with popcorn and cookies in the evening. Rooms have refrigerators (great for chilling the bottle of white wine you purchased from nearby La Dolce Vita Winery) and microwaves. Rooms with hot tubs can be requested. Dogs 20 pounds and under are welcome with a $10 fee per pet per night.

BEST BITES

THE AMERICAN BOUNTY RESTAURANT AND WINE BAR

For mouthwatering burgers and steaks, succulent seafood, and homemade stone-hearth oven-baked pizzas, visit American Bounty at 430 W. Front Street in Washington. Numerous wines, along with single malt scotch options, beer, and specialty martinis don the menu of this popular restaurant where you can dine at one of the sidewalk tables or on the patio with your pooch while listening to live music in warmer months. Boxed meals to-go are also available for purchase.

AUGUSTA BREWING CO.

Click on www.augustabrewing.com and one of the first things you'll see is **"Pets are always welcome!"** While more brewery than winery, Augusta Brewing Co. has eighteen wines to choose from and is a great pub in the midst of wine country. They offer a full menu of appetizers, burgers, salads, and sandwiches for lunch, as well as ribs, seafood, pasta, and beef tenderloin for dinner. Belly up to the outdoor bar and grab a cold glass of their flagship beer, the Tannhauser, a fresh-brewed Rocket Root Beer, or one of the many other beverages offered at 5521 Water Street in Augusta. For a full list of musical entertainment, visit their website.

LOVE DOGS, MUST TRAVEL: BEST OF MISSOURI

SOUTHWEST REGION

BRANSON

Referred to as the "live music capital of the universe" by *60 Minutes* back in the 1990s, Branson continues to live up to the title with its big personalities and countless theaters. Silver Dollar City, Dolly Parton's Dixie Stampede, and the more recently added Titanic Museum, among numerous other family-friendly tourist attractions, continue to draw visitors from all over the country. However, there's more to this town than just bright lights and fast-paced action.

Situated amongst the Ozark Mountains along Lake Taneycomo and Table Rock Lake, Branson is a bustling town nestled in the midst of Mother Nature. A contrasting combination of kitschy tourist attractions and the great outdoors, Branson offers its canine visitors fishing and hiking by day and deluxe accommodations by night, along with some other pretty unique activities. "Better than a bone" restaurants and plush places to stay welcome pooch palates and worn-out paws. Step away from the sparkling lights and over-the-top characters long enough to sniff out the really good stuff Branson has waiting for you.

What Not to Doo Doo

While exploring Table Rock Lake and its surrounding areas, be sure to steer clear of the large and extremely popular Moonshine Beach where many flock to swim and soak up the sun. As inviting as the beckoning cool, clear water might look for a dog paddle or for a few thirst-quenching laps, dogs are not allowed on the sandy shore no matter how well behaved they may be.

PARKS & TRAILS FOR TAILS

CHAD A. FUQUA MEMORIAL PARK

Named after the much-loved and respected longtime Hollister parks director who was tragically killed in an accident, this park is not only a tribute to Chad Fuqua, but it is also a serene and peaceful place to reflect and unwind with your dog. Park benches scatter the .6-mile flat walking trail (ideal for any age or size of dog) and a perfectly placed gazebo offers a shady reprieve from the sun's rays or even a light rain. A lovingly placed statue of a young boy with his black pup and a bench reconstructed from original materials used to build the old St. James Street Bridge decorate this tranquil park designed to bring joy to residents and visitors of Hollister. Just a short scenic drive from the hub of downtown Branson, this park sits on the north side of Hollister Town Hall at 312 Esplanade Street.

DOGWOOD CANYON NATURE PARK

A natural gem in the southern Missouri town of Lampe, this wilderness park spills over the state line into Arkansas. Breathtaking views abound around every corner of the 6.5-mile paved trail that follows the canyon floor. You and your dog can admire the flowing waterfalls, limestone bluffs, caves, and an Amish covered bridge. Don't be surprised if you encounter some form of wildlife, especially if visiting in the morning. Ticket prices are $12.95 for adults, $8.95 for kids between the ages of 3-11, and $2.95 for each dog, with a limit of two. Children two years and under are free. Don't forget to grab a brochure that explains the history of the canyon and tells about the artifacts found on the grounds, including the oldest human remains ever to be found in the state of Missouri. If you prefer your cabins rustic, you'll be happy to know that pets are welcome with a pricey fee of $100 a night and a signed dog waiver form. Information about accommodations, directions, and a full list of dog rules can be found on the website at www.dogwoodcanyon.org.

Fido Fact

Once a small black lab headed for "the end," Pepper's story, thankfully, has a happy ending. Often traveling around as co-pilot in the front seat of an RV playfully referred to as "the dog house" and eating ice cream nightly, Pepper's tale could have been much different. At only a few weeks old, Pepper was to be euthanized, but Chad Fuqua (then Hollister's parks director) took one look at her chewing on Dr. Pepper cans on the floorboard of his truck, and a new friendship was born. Apparently, the little lab liked Dr. Pepper too; thus, Fuqua affectionately named her Pepper. Pepper was often seen riding around with Chad in his truck. Pepper's fate became uncertain again with the unexpected death of Chad, but the dog found a new home with Chad's mother and her husband, Brian. Wanting something good to stem from tragedy, Chad's family, friends, and co-workers created Pepper Dog Park in honor of the loving relationship that both Chad and Pepper had established with Hollister. While Chad's mom, Vonnie Mathiesen, will tell you that "the best thing about the park is the history," other attributes of this park also make it a worthwhile playful venture for you and your loyal companion. While Chad rescued Pepper, it was Pepper who rescued Vonnie after the unexpected loss of her son. Keep an eye out for Pepper riding shotgun in "the dog house," playing in the city parks, or possibly even dressed in character for a local celebration.

PEPPER DOG PARK

Pepper Dog Park is conveniently located just a few minutes from Branson Landing at the corner of Evergreen and Laurel streets. There is no fee to visit this off-leash park and both the small dog side and the one directly attached for larger friends to play in have water and waste stations. Pepper Dog Park is the first of its kind in the area and was designed to offer a safe and family-friendly environment as it sits near other park equipment and frequently used ball courts.

TABLE ROCK LAKE STATE PARK

Nestled within the White River Valley, Table Rock Lake State Park welcomes millions of visitors annually. This area, first inhabited by Native Americans around 10,000 years ago, offers you and your faithful companion endless opportunities for outdoor fun. To generate hydroelectric power and control flooding, Table Rock Dam was built in the 1950s, in turn creating the eight hundred-mile shoreline of Table Rock Lake. Named after a rock shelf sitting high above the White River, this lake is a popular destination for boaters and fishermen, especially those looking to catch bass.

While pontoons and fishing boats are available for rent, so are kayaks, wave runners, and catamarans. With its clear water, scuba diving is not an uncommon sight to see here. **Daredevil dogs** looking for a little more excitement can engage in parasailing, for what's sure to be the best seat in the house for a view of Branson!

Table Rock Lakeshore Trail meanders along the lake and can be accessed from the Dewey Short Visitor Center, the picnic area within the park, and also the *Branson Belle Showboat* (seasonally). Even pups that tend to stay near their owners must be leashed, and as always, owners are required to pick up after them. Built in 2004, Lakeshore Trail meets ADA requirements and has both restrooms and picnic areas on-site. To rent a boat or to schedule your hot dog's parasailing ride, call the Table Rock Lake State Park Marina at 417-334-2628.

SIGHTS & EVENTS WORTH A LICK

BRANSON GHOST & LEGENDS WALKING TOURS

Unlike many attractions in Branson, well-behaved dogs are more than welcome on this one-mile, ninety-minute walking tour that focuses on the early history of Branson and the Ozarks. According to one tour owner, pets often see or sense things that humans cannot. The tour is age appropriate for all, though those 17 years and under must be accompanied by an adult. Children 6 years and under are free, with fees of $20 for adults and $11 for 7-12 year-olds. Bring your camera and let your hound sniff out the spirits of Branson for a howling good time.

BRANSON LANDING FOUNTAINS

The Branson Landing offers something for every type of visitor: from shops and places to dine to street performers and special events. However, the $7.5 million Branson Landing Fountains are the main attraction, with passersby stopping to take in the mesmerizing combination of blasting geysers, colorful lights, playful music, and real fire shooting from cannons. The entrancing display is a show all its own and free to watch for as long as you like. These first-of-their-kind fountains start their engaging display at noon and start over every hour. Go ahead and take a seat, as you're going to want to stay awhile. If your dog is easily startled by loud noises, be sure to sit toward the back and hold her close. Wonderful by day, and more beautiful at night, this is something worth doing twice. Go to www.bransonlanding.com for seasonal show schedules and other current happenings on the landing.

BUSTER'S OLD TIME PHOTOS

Ever wonder what your pup would look like in a Southern belle floppy or ten-gallon hat? Well, you can find out at this pawsitively perfect stop where both you and your canine companion can smile for the camera in fashions from the olden days. Fido might not be the only pet dressing up in period clothing though. According to one employee here, they've photographed all types of animals, from a ferret, to birds, and even a snake. At Buster's Old Time Photos at 211 Branson Landing Boulevard, your dog is encouraged to show his teeth and steal the show.

WHERE TO SIT & STAY

BIG CEDAR LODGE

Follow the winding roads ten miles south of Branson to 612 Devil's Pool Road, Ridgedale. Exquisite views and cascading waterfalls await your arrival. While the $100 pet fee seems steep, one glance at this top-notch facility is guaranteed to convince you that it's worth every penny. If you're looking for a secluded and private vacation spot where you and Fido can take leisurely walks or just sit back and enjoy the company of Mother Nature while the kids go full-speed ahead, then this is the place for you.

There are full-service marinas, stables for pony and carriage rides, an indulgent spa, an arcade, golf courses, a fitness center, several eateries, and outdoor activities to please the whole family.

There are thirteen pet-friendly rooms at the lodge, and while dogs are only allowed in designated areas, there are nearby trails for hiking and **Dogwood Canyon** is just minutes away. Visit www.big-cedar.com for all the great qualities of Big Cedar Lodge. However, the extraordinary kind of beauty which surrounds Big Cedar must be experienced in person to be fully appreciated.

CHATEAU ON THE LAKE RESORT SPA & CONVENTION CENTER

Located on the quieter side of Branson at 415 N. State Highway 265, this five-star hotel accommodates **smaller dogs only** (up to twenty-five pounds) with a $25 fee. With a long list of amenities—tennis courts, indoor and outdoor pools, a hot tub, a 24-hour fitness center, restaurants, a theater, and a full-service marina and spa—your mutt might never want to leave. Fishing, ski, and pontoon boats can be rented, while canoes, kayaks, and paddleboats are offered to guests at no charge. Grab a picnic lunch from the deli or a sinful treat from the Sweet Shoppe and head outside to explore the trails on the property, where your mutt may catch the scent of a deer or even glimpse a wild turkey or armadillo. Pet rooms are conveniently located on the third floor, and rooms with a view of the lake or mountains can be requested. With rates as low as $110 in the off-season, you can pamper your pet and yourself.

HILTON PROMENADE AT BRANSON LANDING

Although the design is contemporary and modern, this lakeside hotel is quite warm and inviting and just mere steps from all the fun that Branson Landing has waiting for you. At minimum you'll want to request a room with a view of Lake Taneycomo or the fountain show on the Landing. However, extra-pampered pooches will expect their humans to reserve a suite or condo with private balcony where they can sniff it all out. Pups up to seventy-five pounds are welcome to **lap up this luxury** with their owners for a well-spent $50 nonrefundable fee. While situated in the midst of all the excitement Branson has to offer, you'll feel worlds away from all the activity once tucked away in your quiet room. Amenities abound, with an indoor and outdoor pool, restaurant, and bar. Booking early can save guests up to 20 percent off the best available pricing (3 Branson Landing; www3.hilton.com).

HOMEAWAY.COM

There are endless options on homeaway.com for travelers heading to Branson with their pets. Although many of the resorts do require a minimum of two or three nights stay and some are a bit further from popular attractions, a condo, cabin, or resort is a great option for **large families with pets.** Several of these properties can accommodate numbers in the teens or more, and often can group several units together. Most of the resorts and condominium complexes offer access to pools, playgrounds, walking areas, and other amenities. This option can save visitors money on meals (as most have full kitchens or outdoor grilling areas) and room rates, provide more generous living spaces to gather, and still allow for the privacy of separate bedrooms and bathrooms. Because many of the properties are privately owned, guests may be more likely to receive discounts or special accommodations. Be sure to get a signed contract and check popular websites for recent reviews of the properties.

BEST BITES

DAVE'S FAMOUS BARBEQUE

Dishing up award-winning ribs and other meats perfectly smoked and sauced, Dave's Famous Barbeque is at 1201 Branson Landing. Choose from classics like the Georgia chopped pork, feasts that include a little bit of everything served on a garbage can lid, and lunch and early bird specials. You and your pooch can kick back with some barbeque on Dave's laidback patio or get it to-go.

DINO'S 24 KARROT CAKE CAFÉ

Bring your dog and eat cake too. Watch the strolling shoppers from the lovely front patio at 307 Branson Landing where you and your furry friend can indulge in what many claim is the best carrot cake in the world. There's also the Italian crème (downright sinful), the red velvet (to die for), the coconut (melts-in-your-mouth good), and the list goes on and on. Owner Dino Kartsonakis is well known as a pianist around the world, having won a Grammy and countless Gospel Music Awards and still performs in Branson. He first tried his cakes out on his musician friends such as Tony Orlando, and celebrity fans include Denzel Washington, Billy Graham, and Mike Huckabee, who have his cakes shipped directly to them. Dino's offers cinnamon rolls, muffins, and turnovers for breakfast too. Specialty coffee drinks, including Dino's signature blend of coffee, make a fine companion for your sweet treat any time of day.

TEXAS LAND & CATTLE STEAK HOUSE

One of only a few restaurants where you can settle in to watch the famous Branson Landing fountains from a front-row patio seat, this establishment also serves up some mouthwatering grub. Munch on some onion straws or fried jalapeños for starters, slurp up some smoked chicken tortilla soup, bite into a juicy steak (don't forget your furry friend under the table), or savor a salmon filet marinated in soy sauce and Sam Adams Boston Lager. Unexpected standouts speckle the menu, such as the mesquite-grilled quail and Cajun ribeye for the more adventurous diner. Top it all off with a slice of the bourbon pecan pie or triple chocolate miracle cake. Afterwards, walk it off with a leisurely stroll through the Landing area. For a complete list of tantalizing menu items, visit www.texaslandandcattle.com. Texas Land & Cattle is located at 915 Branson Landing Boulevard.

VINTAGE PARIS COFFEE & WINE CAFÉ

As parents of two rescues (a dog named Rosie and a cat named Saki), the owners of Vintage Paris **highly encourage all pets** to enjoy the lovely courtyard with their humans and love to have furry visitors. Savor some rich Askinosie chocolate with a gourmet coffee or one of the many varieties of wines offered at this quaint café. Beers from around the world are also available along with a limited but enticing café menu of sandwiches and delightful desserts from local bakers. To-go water bowls are provided, but since Fido can't have chocolate or alcohol, it might be wise to bring him a doggie bag of goodies. The Vintage Paris Coffee & Wine Café is located at 260 Bird Cage Walk in Hollister, just down from the Chad A. Fuqua Memorial Park.

SOUTHWEST REGION

CARTHAGE

Slow down the pace and take a step back into yesteryear with a trip to Carthage. With three districts listed on the National Register of Historic Places, in addition to other buildings around town, you will want to dive into the town's somewhat surprising past. Like many other towns of Missouri, Carthage had to be rebuilt after the Civil War. However, it then became a thriving community—socially, agriculturally, and in the coal mining business. Though her population is over fourteen thousand today, Carthage maintains a small-town feel combined with natural beauty, eye-catching architecture, and interesting facts of days gone by. Travelers might easily overlook this far southwest Missouri town—appropriately referred to as "Little City Among the Trees" and "The Open Gate to the Ozarks"—but a visit is worth the effort.

Battle of Carthage State Historic Site

PARKS & TRAILS FOR TAILS

CENTRAL PARK

Although since moved to a different site, this area at West Seventh Street was once the original burial grounds for the casualties of the Battle of Carthage. Redeveloped as Central Park in 1871, it is now a popular destination for tourists and locals alike. Unique features to the park are the sculpture of Zoologist Marlin Perkins, the 1930s wading pool and bathhouse, and a memorial honoring Missouri's fallen Vietnam veterans. Playgrounds and picnic areas complete the park.

KELLOGG LAKE

Just east of Carthage and right off Old Route 66 (now Highway 96) at 1215 Esterly Drive, Kellogg Lake is an ideal spot for fishing and hiking with your dog. Pack a picnic lunch so you can immerse yourselves in the area's tranquil setting and take your time to explore the species and plant life unique to the region. Admission is free, and visitors are welcome from dawn to dusk.

SIGHTS & EVENTS WORTH A LICK

BATTLE OF CARTHAGE STATE HISTORIC SITE

The now-quiet open meadow and spring was once the ending location of the Civil War's first full-scale battle, fought on July 5, 1861. The battle site sits in Carthage off East Chestnut Street next to Carter Park, where the park's gates are a memorial to the Battle of Carthage and other minor battles. The seven-acre site encompasses the Carter Springs area and an interpretational kiosk that allows visitors to follow the battle from its beginning to a Confederate victory. The site is open from dawn to dusk with no admission (www.mostateparks.com). Pick up a history guide from the Carthage Convention & Visitors' Bureau to map out and tour other Carthage battle markers of the Civil War, such as Quarry Hill and the area just south of Dry Fork Bridge.

KENDRICK PLACE

Built in the 1850s, the Kendrick house is the oldest home in Jasper County and was inhabited by the Kendrick family for more than 125 years, although they were not the original owners. During the Civil War, the Kendricks opened their door to fighters of both the North and South, and this neutrality may be why it was one of the few houses to survive the war. Unfortunately, canines are not allowed inside Kendrick Place. However, it's worth a drive by this antebellum home due to the historic tales and rumors of paranormal. Maybe your pup will see or sense something to make him howl. Tours are available for humans, and many special events are held here.

No Bones About It

SOUTHWEST REGION: CARTHAGE

MAPLE LEAF FESTIVAL

During the Maple Leaf Festival, be sure to catch the **Community Dog Show** in Carthage Square in front of City Hall, which is free to watch and to enter. Also free to spectators is the Maple Leaf K-9 Leap & Dash, sponsored by Central Pet Care and held in Municipal Park within the Jasper County Fairgrounds. Call the Chamber of Commerce at 417-358-2373 for more information or to register your competitor. Don't miss the Maple Leaf Parade, which begins at Historic Carthage Square. Please visit www.CarthageMapleLeaf.com.

PRECIOUS MOMENTS CHAPEL & GARDENS

Whether a collector or not, travelers must stop and see this special tribute to the well-known Precious Moments figurines. Stroll along the Avenue of Angels or sit by the serene water of Center Creek to feel the calming influence of the many acres of grounds decorated with fountains and countless varieties of flowers and plants. Visitors will find it difficult to hurry through this haven of happiness. While only humans are allowed within the buildings, if possible, visitors should partake in the chapel tour (inspired by the Sistine Chapel in Rome and Samuel J. Butcher's own faith), where Butcher's depiction of the Old and New Testaments meet in breathtaking hand-painted murals. There is a café and gift shop on the property where shoppers can purchase exclusive pieces found nowhere else. The gardens are open year-round except for a few holidays. All the glorious details of the Precious Moments Park and Chapel are at www.preciousmoments.com.

RED OAK II

Experience the buildings of old in a new location. Saddened by the ghost town his hometown of Red Oak had become after returning in the 1970s, artist Lowell Davis started buying up the homes and businesses, moving them to his land off County Loop 122, and restoring them to their original conditions, thus creating Red Oak II. Old vehicles and sculptures by Davis are located throughout the property while a path leads to a church, 1920s-style Phillips 66 gas station, Belle Starr's home (the original home of the infamous lady outlaw where Davis now lives), and other country village buildings. Red Oak II is a charming little stroll into the days of yore unique to Carthage. For directions and a listing of current events at Red Oak II, visit the official website (www.redoakiimissouri.com).

VICTORIAN HOME DRIVING TOUR

The perfect all-weather (and *free*) activity in Carthage, which you and your pooch can enjoy from your car, is the self-guided Victorian Home Driving Tour. Leisurely meander through one of Missouri's largest historic districts while admiring the lovely architecture of private homes, all built between 1870 and 1910. These significant homes were the result of the mining boom and the numerous resulting millionaires living in Carthage at that time. For maps of the tour, stop by 402 S. Garrison Avenue.

PuppyPicks

66 Drive-In Theatre

Rain or shine between the months of April and September, take in dinner and a movie at an old-fashioned drive-in theatre. Outside food is allowed, but they prefer to have customers purchase from the concession stand. No alcohol is allowed and only cash is accepted. Ticket prices range from $3-7, with children five and under getting in free. The last of six drive-in theatres named after Route 66, this blast-from-the-past attraction can be found at 17231 Old 66 Boulevard. For a list of shows playing and directions, visit www.66drivein.com or call 417-359-5959. Encourage Fido to follow puppy etiquette so everyone can enjoy the double feature.

WHERE TO SIT & STAY

BEST WESTERN PRECIOUS MOMENTS HOTEL

For a truly unique overnight experience, stay at the Best Western, which was designed and decorated by Precious Moments creator Samuel J. Butcher. Original pieces of Butcher's work—such as silk screens and exclusive paintings—can be admired throughout the hotel. Standard rooms start at a little over $75 a night and king, executive, and even two-story loft suites are also available. Amenities include an indoor heated pool, a free buffet breakfast, and free parking. Some suites also have whirlpool spa tubs, and there is a gift shop within the hotel. Two pets up to eighty pounds are allowed for just $10 a night. Be sure to call ahead, as pet rooms are based on availability and some breed restrictions may apply. Three miles from the Precious Moments Park and Chapel, the Best Western is located at 2701 Hazel Street (www.bestwestern.com; 800-511-7676).

BEST BITES

WHISLER'S HAMBURGERS

There are numerous popular fast food options such as Gringo's, Sonic, Braum's, and Subway in Carthage. However, for a truly original experience, visitors must order an old-fashioned hamburger from Whisler's at 300 N. Garrison Avenue. To pork it up a bit, order the Pig & Bull (hamburger with ham), Sow & Cow (hamburger with bacon), or the Farm (a hamburger with both ham and bacon). In business since 1953, Whisler's also offers shakes and floats, soda, chips, and candy—all with a friendly smile. Head inside to order and sit outside at one of the picnic tables. Better yet, get it to-go for a picnic lunch at Kellogg Lake.

SOUTHWEST REGION

SPRINGFIELD

Today, the bustling college town of Springfield, at times still referred to as the "Queen City of the Ozarks," is a delightful mix of sites, shops, eateries, numerous parks, and even a few "one of a kind" activities for visitors to enjoy with their dogs. It is difficult to imagine the once-bloody battlefields of the Civil War that occurred on her lush grounds and rolling hills. There are many historic sites, legendary moments, and stories about soldiers from both the Confederate and Union armies.

The first-recorded shootout took place on the town square in Springfield between Wild Bill Hickok and Davis Tutt, after a poker game where the two had a disagreement over whether or not Hickok owed Tutt money. The duel was considered the first of its kind because both shooters faced each other sideways instead of the typical face-to-face stance. Tutt actually fired first but missed. Hickok shot and killed him.

In addition, Springfield is known as the birthplace of Historic Route 66. Springfield is a great city for those of all ages to explore, including families with young kids and the family dog in tow.

PARKS & TRAILS FOR TAILS

CRUSE DOG PARK

With 4.5 enclosed acres for large dogs and 1.5 acres dedicated to small dogs, Cruse Dog Park is well maintained, large, and ideal for your furry friend to romp and play. Three-tier water fountains (found in both the large and small enclosed play areas) are perfect for dogs as well as humans, and waste stations are provided. Visitors can purchase a daily pass for $10 per dog and are limited to two dogs per owner (be sure to bring a copy of current vaccinations from your vet). If you're planning to visit several times during your stay, the annual fee of $25 may be a more sensible purchase. The address is 2100 W. Catalpa, which is where GPS will direct you. However, for the main entrance and parking, you'll want to enter off Grand and Kansas Expressway. Your dog will love visiting Springfield's first off-leash park and might even encourage you to walk the nearby trail with him or her.

SEQUIOTA PARK

Originally treaty land awarded to the Delaware Native Americans after the Louisiana Purchase, Sequiota Park sits at 3500 S. Lone Pine Avenue and offers its guests twenty-eight acres in which to explore. Let your pup take you for a walk on the three-mile fitness and walking trail or just sit by the duck pond and decompress. The park offers visitors both children's and adult play equipment, grills, picnic tables, open shelters, restrooms, and a water fountain all in a serene natural setting. Sequiota Park makes a great stop before or after Creek Side Bistro (just down the way) and Galloway Ice Cream Shoppe, which is located across the street from the park. For a complete list of the many parks in Springfield, visit www.springfieldparks.org.

SPRINGFIELD CONSERVATION NATURE CENTER TRAILS

What Not to Doo Doo

The Springfield Conservation Trails are a series of trails, bodies of water, natural lands, and a Nature Center within the city limits. Activities and displays are year-round within the Nature Center, and there is much to be discovered in the natural settings that surround the trail areas. While a great way to get exercise outdoors and observe nature, understandably, your furry pal is not allowed on these grounds. In order to conserve wildlife, natural habitats, and plant life, the area is also closed to horses, bicyclists, roller bladers, skaters, and motorized vehicles. Throw your dog a bone and leave this activity for another time when your pooch is not traveling with you.

SIGHTS & EVENTS WORTH A LICK

BARK IN THE PARK

For more than twenty years this annual festival has been a great way to bring dogs and their families out to enjoy canine activities together while supporting Cruse Dog Park. Presented by both Nathanael Greene County Park Board and the Citizens Dog Park Committee, this June event includes a **dog talent show,** a guided dog walk, crafts, and a **canine vendor village** featuring commercial and non-profit organizations and retailers. A registration fee of just $10 comes with a T-shirt for yourself. You can register the day of the event at Nathanael Greene-Close Memorial Park at 2400 S. Scenic Avenue. While there, be sure to take in the view of the beautiful Botanical Gardens, which are generously maintained by volunteers, and check out the unique Japanese stroll garden.

BARK IN THE PARK AT HAMMONS FIELD

You certainly won't strike out when you take your best companion to the ball game for America's favorite pastime! Once a year in the spring, Hammons Field, home to the AA Springfield Cardinals, **welcomes dogs** and their owners to the park for a fun-filled night of baseball. Ticket prices range from $6 for grass seats (a good option if your dog is larger or a bit rowdy) to $47. Lap dogs are welcome to sit on their owners' laps in the stadium seats. Much of the proceeds go to the Humane Society, which is typically on hand to show off their adoptable friends in need of a good home. Your mutt will surely want to strut his stuff on the field in the parade and enjoy the pre-game activities, so be sure to arrive early. Then grab a dog (hot dog, that is) and settle in for a night that's sure to be a home run. You will be required to sign a waiver upon entering the park to ensure responsibility for your pet and that you will clean up after him. Please explain to your dog that she should leave the pop flies to you and that this ball isn't for chasing. For current pricing and details, call 417-863-0395.

CIDER DAYS

This annual fall festival is a regional artists' and crafters' haven with handmade jewelry, pottery, glass, woodwork, and other treasures for sale. Grab some hot apple cider and let your paws hit the pavement of Historic Walnut Street, where you're sure to encounter many other furry friends. Local musicians will entertain while the local cuisine is guaranteed to please your palate. In addition, the comedy improv and obstacle races are always a big hit. With kids' activities such as face painting, inflatables, and the scarecrow village, you may have trouble pulling the younger ones away from the children's area to move on to the next feature or artisan demonstration. Hours are 10-5 each day and admission is $4, with children 10 and under free. Many thousands—locals and tourists alike—attend every year, so you'll want to arrive early.

DOG FEST

If you happen to be visiting Springfield in September, your pooch could end up with a busier social calendar than you! The annual Dog Fest is held at Chesterfield Park (2511 W. Republic Road) and features vendors, pet products (cute clothing, treats, photography), and non-profit organizations. A favorite of the event is the **Dachshund Dash,** where wiener dogs prove who is the "Best of the Best." Even an underdog can be a champion with the Best of the Worst Award. The event is free, and proceeds benefit Cruse Dog Park.

DOG SWIM

Also in September, the annual evening Dog Swim at Fassnight Outdoor Pool (located at 1300 S. Campbell) is always a popular event. Dogs must have proof of all vaccinations, and each owner is **limited to one dog.** There is a minimal fee and pre-registration is strongly recommended (www.parkboard.org). Your pup will have fun splashing around with water mates, and 100 percent of the proceeds go to Cruse Dog Park.

FANTASTIC CAVERNS

Open daily aside from Thanksgiving Day, Christmas Eve, and Christmas Day, Fantastic Caverns is a truly original experience that you and your pooch can have together. Maintaining a temperature of about 60 degrees year-round, the caverns offer the perfect activity for any day of the year. Before or after the tour, you'll want to take in the beautiful surroundings of the hiking trail that leads to a collapsed cave, river valley, and natural spring. The now ride-through cave featuring stalactites, stalagmites, soda straws, and glistening flowstones was discovered accidentally by a farmer's dog in 1862. The tour lasts nearly an hour, with guides providing information about the origin of the formations, species of wildlife inhabiting the cave (many of which are now endangered), and environmental lessons. Be sure to let your guide know you are packing a pal on the tour and he will give you top-notch seats. Check out www.fantasticcaverns.com for hours and rates.

OOVVDA WINERY

Owner Brian Overboe is half Norwegian, a fourth Swedish, and a fourth British with his family tree dating back to 1189. OOVVDA is an acronym for "Overboes' Own Viking Vintners Distinctive Alcohols," pronounced from the homonym for *Uff da*, an all-purpose Norwegian or Scandinavian word (check out the many definitions adapted for this word since the nineteenth century on wikipedia,

Fido Fact

In 1862, John Knox's hunting dog slipped through a narrow opening to the cave that is known today as Fantastic Caverns. It is believed that Knox kept his knowledge of the cave a secret for many years to avoid the Confederates or Union from using it as a possible source for saltpeter. Five years after finding the cave, Knox put an ad in the paper asking for someone to explore it. Surprisingly, a group of twelve women from a Springfield athletic club answered the ad and were the inaugural spelunkers. The names of these women were inscribed on a wall inside the cave and can still be seen today. Interestingly, the caverns weren't always used just for viewing. During Prohibition, the caverns were used as a speakeasy, and during the 1950s and 1960s, music concerts were held there. Shows were even broadcast on the radio in the 1970s. Knox's dog probably had no idea just how fantastic his discovery would become.

where you'll even find mention of OOVVDA Winery). Don't be surprised if Ashley, the **friendly resident collie** (part border, part Australian), greets you upon arrival. Just ten minutes from I-44 and US 65, OOVVDA Winery is the perfect place to kick back with your furry friend on a sunny afternoon. Both tastings and tours are complimentary, and while the winery doesn't have a food license, they offer barbeque grills for guests to use during their visit. The ever-popular Semi-Sweet Chambourcin, unique Peach-Melba, a combination of raspberry and peach with a drop of vanilla, and dry Tomato are just a few of the many and unique wines you can sample here. Be sure to call ahead or check the website for the musical entertainment schedule (417-833-4896, www.oovvda.com).

PETS & PUMPKINS

Your pet will love getting dressed up in costume for the **pet parade** at this annual event on Commercial Street, a vibrant shopping and entertainment district known as C-street to the locals, sponsored by *Tame Magazine*. Aside from the parade and contests, there is live music, lots of food (including marshmallow roasting), and inflatables for your non-furry kids to enjoy. All proceeds are donated to local non-profits working toward saving the lives of homeless animals and educating the public about pet population. Whether you're trying to win the Best Pet/Owner Combo Award by donning complementary costumes such as Little Red Riding Hood and the Big Bad Wolf or are hoping for an award in another category, you will see just about every type of costume. Do tricks and get treats at Pets & Pumpkins to support a most worthy cause!

WILSON'S CREEK NATIONAL BATTLEFIELD

Just southwest of Springfield, at 6424 W. Farm Road 182, is Wilson's Creek National Battlefield, where the Civil War in western Missouri began in 1861. The 4.9-mile auto tour complete with audio messages allows you to explore the major battlefield points and learn about the Confederate and Union commanders of that time. Along the tour you will find exhibits, maps, a historic overlook, and even trails where you and your pup can explore historic ground. There is a fee for the tour and dogs must remain on leashes at all times. The Visitors' Center offers a bookstore, demonstrations, videos, and restrooms; however, dogs are not allowed inside the building. Whether walking one of the many trails or driving the battlefield tour, this is another great activity that you and your canine companion can do together at any time of the year.

WHERE TO SIT & STAY

UNIVERSITY PLAZA & CONVENTION CENTER

The University Plaza & Convention Center is just down the street from Hammons Field, at 333 S. John Q. Hammons Parkway. If your pup is missing her fish friends from home (and won't think it's a treat) or you aren't traveling with your dog, request a goldfish to keep you company. While not as cuddly as your furry friend, it's a bonus feature of this hotel. With an on-site restaurant serving a complimentary breakfast buffet each morning, lounge, fitness center, indoor and outdoor pools, whirlpool, sundeck, and gift shop, you'll have everything you need. Parking is complimentary and laundry facilities are available. Water and food bowls along with waste-disposal bags are provided for your pet's stay, as well as a **pet bed** upon request. A reasonable $25 non-refundable fee is required. To book your pet-package stay, go to www.upspringfield.com

PuppyPicks

KOA Campground

"**Ruffing**" it never felt so good! Awarded the distinctive KOA President's Award in 2012, the KOA campground at 5775 W. Farm Road 140 in Springfield will exceed your expectations. Fido will lick your face up one side and down the other for bringing him to the campground with Kamp K-9, the off-leash dog park complete with a miniature log cabin and teeter totter. The grounds are meticulous with open grassy areas, a pool, playground, tetherball, volleyball, a basketball hoop, and horseshoe pit. The campground offers something for everyone with four-to-six-person cabins and deluxe cabins, RV sites, and places to pitch a tent. Request the lodge with a deck, one with a screened-in porch, or even the one named "Hound Dog Molly" to make your pooch feel right at home. Find all your camping needs along with snacks, pizza, and bike rentals on-site. For cabin models, a site map, and a complete list of services, visit www.koa.com/campgrounds/springfield-route-66 or call 417-831-3645.

LOVE DOGS, MUST TRAVEL: BEST OF MISSOURI

WALNUT STREET INN (COTTAGE INN GUEST ROOMS)

A self-proclaimed urban oasis in downtown Springfield, the Walnut Street Inn was voted best Bed & Breakfast in the Ozarks four years in a row by *Springfield News Leader* readers. Located in the historic district where Victorian architecture is prevalent, the inn is close enough to walk to the happening downtown area where you're sure to run into lots of other four-legged friends. When you call Walnut Street Inn, be sure to request the Finley Suite or Jordan Room, both of which are pet friendly and located in the Cottage Inn, just two doors east of the Walnut Street Inn. Both the Finley suite, which is quite large and named after Finley River, and the Jordan Room (named for Jordan Creek) boast queen feather beds (the feather top is removable upon request), gas fireplaces, WiFi access, stocked beverage bars, and coffeemakers. The Finley also has an over-sized chair that folds out into a twin-sized bed for an additional guest, a jet tub for two and a separate walk-in shower. The Jordan Room is complete with a two-person steam shower. The Cottage Inn has a nice yard for walking your pup, and both the Jordan Valley and Phelps Grove parks are within walking distance. There is a $20 non-refundable pet fee and pets must be well behaved, but there is no discrimination against larger dogs. Owners must sign a waiver upon arrival and are required to crate their pups if left alone in the room. Prop your paws up on the porch and enjoy the privacy and seclusion of the Cottage Inn ($149-179, www.walnutstreetinn.com).

BEST BITES

BAMBINO'S

Tucked away in the cozy neighborhood of Phelps Grove at 1141 E. Delmar, local favorite Bambino's offers great service, downright yummy fare, and a welcoming patio for your dog. The patio has both covered and uncovered seating. Mouth-watering pastas dominate the fairly priced menu, but paninis, soups and salads, pizzas, appetizers, and desserts are also available for lunch or dinner. Be sure to ask about the daily specials, which are also posted at www.bambinoscafe.com. This cuisine is worth getting off the beaten path (the broccoli cheese soup is super creamy).

THE BLUE BULL BAR & GRILL

Opt for a front patio table at downtown hot spot Blue Bull Bar & Grill to watch the action on the square while enjoying one of their famous burgers or other menu items. While the Signature Blue Bull Burger with a pretzel bun is always a good choice, the Blue Flame Burger is perfect for those who like theirs a bit hot and spicy. Each martini concoction is more tantalizing than the next and so tempting that you must indulge, but beware! Lap up too much and you'll need the **hair of the dog** in the morning. Sip an Angel on Acid, the Jungle Boogie, a Hpnotiq Breeze, or one of the many other flavors from the extensive martini list. In addition to burgers, Blue Bull offers appetizers, wraps (try the steak with cilantro ranch dressing), salads, chicken sandwiches of all varieties, and even tenderloin, so there's something to whet everyone's appetite. Blue Bull Bar & Grill is located at 105 Park Central Square and is open six days a week.

THE COFFEE ETHIC

For the perfect brew (beer or grounds) with the perfect view, head over to the Coffee Ethic at 124 Park Central Square. Choose one of the many rotating beers on tap while enjoying live music or other activities on the square from the front patio. After you order up an individually brewed coffee drink, tea, or smoothie you can sit back to relax while the sounds of the busy downtown area perk up your pup's ears. A small selection of wine is also offered, along with a few tasty breakfast items. Later hours make this a great evening stop as well. Recycled, sustainable materials make for an earthy yet cool modern interior where the service is friendly and the aromas divine.

CREEK SIDE BISTRO

The back patio at this quirky bistro (complete with mannequins and old signs) rests on a meandering creek, just down the way from Sequiota Park on Lone Pine and provides an ideal setting to relax with Fido for a cold one and the Bistro's signature homemade tortillas. The few menu items of the day are written on the board inside. Take time out from exploring the city to enjoy a bit of nature while giving your paws a rest. Definitely visit the retailer next door, Inspirational Home, for beautiful and unique items and a section of **products for dog lovers.** I purchased a "Kiss the Dog" sign, which I believe everyone should do often!

GALLOWAY ICE CREAM SHOPPE

When you're done playing at Sequiota Park, lap up a cool treat at Galloway Ice Cream Shoppe across the street at 3521 S. Lone Pine Avenue. Your pup can indulge in a **doggie sundae,** made with a scoop of non-fat vanilla ice cream and topped off with a dog biscuit. They have delicious scoops for humans, too. A water bowl for your pooch is provided so you won't have to bring your own.

THE WING SHACK GRILL & BAR

With plenty of outdoor seating for you and your furry companion, the Wing Shack is only a few blocks from historic Walnut Street and Hammons Field, among other local attractions, which makes it a great option for a casual meal. The teriyaki sauce is downright finger-licking good on the traditional wings, but you can also opt for mild, original hot, buff-a-que, nuclear, sweet bbq, Hawaiian, Caribbean, garlic-Parmesan, and lemon pepper. There's a long list of tempting appetizers and desserts to get you started and finish you off. Steaks, burgers, sandwiches, and wraps round out the menu. The Wing Shack Grill & Bar is located at 307 S. National and is **doggone good.**

RYMAC'S RUB N PUB

Get started with the Skinny Dip Wings or some Mother Cluckers from the appetizer menu and then move on to the Shroomed or Bootlegger burger or sandwich. With eight rubs and eight sauces to choose from, your meal is sure to be barkin'! Dogs are welcome on the patio, and water bowls are available in warmer months. A friendly bark will earn your pooch a complimentary dog biscuit. The food at RyMac's is saucy, and so is the attitude. Check out the lively menu at www.rymacsrubandpub.com and visit them at 107 Park Central Square.

POSH PUPPY

ALL ABOUT DOGS & CATS

Located at 2632 S. Glenstone Avenue, this **pet boutique** has high-quality pet food, their own in-house groomer, and an on-site bakery where they make lip-smacking treats your pooch will want to try. While you're there, pick up some Goodness Gracious jerky treats for your dog or cat. They are healthy, but best of all 51 percent of the profits go to community-based animal charities. Gluten-free products are also available.

ALL PET SUPPLIES & EQUINE CENTER

Pet party supplies, remembrance items, and canine fashion along with toys and pet food are just a few of the things you can purchase at All Pet Supplies & Equine Center. **Pet stylists** are also on hand for all your pup's grooming needs. This locally owned wholesale outlet has locations at 1611 W. Republic Road and 2845 Kearney Street. Harlie and Kaia loved the fresh bakery treats, and the long chicken chew sticks were a huge hit.

SOUTHEAST REGION

ARCADIA VALLEY

Once your stomach gets over the drop it takes every time you descend down one of the rolling hills, you'll be astounded by the beauty that surrounds you on the drive to this three-town gem. Arcadia Valley consists of Pilot Knob (the most northern of the three), Arcadia (the most southern), and Ironton (which sits between the two). With majestic views around every corner, you can easily lose track of time while cruising down these winding roads. Just make sure your pup isn't prone to carsickness! Arcadia Valley shares her serene beauty through her natural parks and trails and engages visitors with her Ozark heritage.

Tracking Tips

While it's easy to let the excitement of exploring a new area overwhelm you, it's a good idea to make the Visitors' Center your first stop in town. In a rural area like this, GPS is not always reliable. When driving through the forest and park areas, it is easy to miss a turn or make a wrong one, and it could take a while before you realize it or find a safe spot to turn around. Study the maps and have a clear plan before you go. The Whistle Junction Visitors' Center & Iron County Historical Society Museum is located at 630 Highway 21 in Arcadia.

PARKS & TRAILS FOR TAILS

ELEPHANT ROCKS STATE PARK

For a less strenuous hike and great photo opportunities, visit Elephant Rocks State Park near Farmington in Graniteville. These large boulders made from crystalline red granite look like elephant feet, with the largest weighing in at 680 tons. The winding Braille Trail accommodates those with physical and visual challenges and is appropriate for all ages and **all types of dogs.** The trail offers visitors a view overlooking the old quarry site, wildlife-watching by the quarry pond, and the option of climbing right up onto the rocks.

JOHNSON'S SHUT-INS STATE PARK

The majority of the park along with about two miles of river frontage was donated by Joseph Desloge in 1955, a truly priceless gift. At over 8,000 acres, Johnson's Shut-Ins State Park encompasses steep forests, mountains, and wetlands, in addition to the overwhelmingly popular shut-ins, which consist of about 180 acres. The park has a gift shop, shuttle system, and several other areas you'll want to see, like Scour Channel Overlook. Reserve a pet-friendly cabin in the park to rest up for the next day's adventures.

What Not to Doo Doo

Canines are allowed everywhere in Johnson's Shut-Ins State Park except on the quarter-mile trail leading to and into the Shut-Ins. Instead, hit the river at the north day-use area where pups are welcome. Pups must remain leashed at all times when in the park.

LOVE DOGS, MUST TRAVEL: BEST OF MISSOURI

TAUM SAUK MOUNTAIN STATE PARK

At 1,772 feet above sea level, Taum Sauk Mountain is the highest point in the state of Missouri and a place where many come to hike, camp, and just absorb the gifts of Mother Nature. For those who want to hit the summit, it's much easier than you might think. Follow the winding roads through the dense forest to the parking lot for Taum Sauk Mountain. From there it's a short paved walk to the summit. A slightly more challenging hike is to Mina Sauk Falls, Missouri's tallest waterfall. If you can handle the three-mile round-trip hike, you'll think it every bit worth the effort once you see and hear the falls. Especially majestic when there's been an abundance of rain, the falls flow generously onto ledges below before finally combining into a pool of clear water. Still visibly scarred today with rhyolite and coarse-grained granite created by volcanic eruptions over a billion years ago, the Devil's Tollgate sits on the Ozark Trail and is thirty feet high on both sides and fifty feet long. For more serious hikers, it is a ten-mile hike from here to Johnson's Shut-Ins State Park. Just down from the state park and high above the valley is the Missouri Department of Conservation–owned lookout tower. From here you can see for miles. Guides are available to help visitors distinguish the abundant wildlife, plants, and nearby mountains. For those who prefer rugged camping there are twelve campsites at this location, along with a picnic site and special use area. Taum Sauk State Park is nine miles southwest of Ironton on Route CC off Highway 21-72. The park is unmanned, so visitors should contact Johnson's Shut-Ins State Park for assistance (573-546-2450).

SIGHTS & EVENTS WORTH A LICK

FORT DAVIDSON STATE HISTORIC SITE

These grounds were the bloody site of the Battle of Pilot Knob, where Confederate troops led by General Sterling Price launched an attack on the Union soldiers. Outnumbered, the Union drew protection from the fort's tall walls, which were surrounded by a dry moat. The Confederates withdrew and made plans to attack the following day. Knowing that they didn't have enough supplies to last another day under attack, the Union soldiers escaped during the night, traveling through Confederate camps as they went. Today, the grounds of Fort Davidson State Historic Site are peaceful, but you can still see the moat around the walls of the fort and the site where the Confederates created a mass grave. Reenactments of the Battle of Pilot Knob still take place at the Fort Davidson State Historic Site. With the year of 2014 marking the 150th anniversary of the end of the Civil War, many additional activities will be taking place then (www.missouri-vacations.com/fort-davidson-state-historic-site).

GENERAL ULYSSES S. GRANT STATUE

While stationed in Arcadia Valley, Grant received his commission as brigadier general where this memorial statue now stands. Honoring the lives of those lost in the Battle of Pilot Knob in 1864 along with Grant, the statue is located on the grounds of Ste. Marie du Lac Church at 350 S. Main in Ironton.

IRON COUNTY COURT HOUSE

The antebellum Iron County Court House sits at 250 S. Main and was built in 1860. It was used as a hospital during the Civil War and is still visibly scarred where it was hit by a cannonball. This building is still used as the Iron County Court House.

PuppyPicks

Self-driving Tour
Numerous battlefield sites significant to the Civil War are located throughout Arcadia Valley. Visitors can explore these battlefields through their own self-driving tour. The historic sites are marked with red granite monuments, and you can pick up a map for the tour at Fort Davidson State Historic Site inside the Visitors' Center.

POPLAR BLUFF

As the gateway to the Ozarks, Poplar Bluff, about eighty miles south of Arcadia, is adjacent to numerous outdoor areas where visitors can romp and play with their furry friends. Mark Twain National Forest is a 150,000-acre playground, and Wappapello Lake lets guests hike, fish, boat, swim, hunt, and camp. With six overlooks and picnic areas, the nineteen-mile self-guided auto tour route of the Mingo National Wildlife Refuge is a great way for you and your pooch to take in the flora and possibly catch a glimpse of some indigenous species. A one-mile self-guided nature trail is also available. True fall foliage seekers should definitely make the Fall Color Driving Tour, which encompasses fifty-six miles and takes about ninety minutes without stops. Drivers can find information about places along the route and download the map at www.visitbutler-countymo.com.

Water-loving dogs will enjoy canoeing, floating, hiking, or swimming at Keener Springs in Williamsville. This sixty-five-acre property is located on the Black River, boasts a water-filled cave, and is one of the largest privately owned springs in the country. Most well-behaved dogs are welcome in the cabins with a refundable $65 deposit. Day passes to visit the area, including the river beach, are just $5 and those five years and under are admitted for free. To book a float trip or reserve a cabin, see www.keenersprings.com.

Indian Hills Winery offers guests good wines from the vine, beautiful views, and a slower pace. Canines are not allowed up on the deck, but are welcome to join their human companions at the tables below and to roam the grounds. The three resident pooches and neighbor pup will likely offer a tail wagging welcome. Indian Hills is open April through October with bistro-type fare during busier months (www.indianhillswinery.com). Eagle Pass Winery is located at 2431 County Road 534 between Lake Wappapello and Poplar Bluff and offers casual fare. Smaller dogs are allowed on the deck. In addition, a 10 x 12-foot fenced area is available where your pup can play while you engage in some wine tasting.

Travelers looking for a bite on the go can visit Hayden's Drive In, get take-out from Mike & Zach's BBQ To-Go, or order carry out at one of the numerous pizza joints or other restaurants in town. Please your pup and picnic together in one of the beautiful settings that abound near Poplar Bluff.

After an exciting day, you and your pooch can both relax at the Drury Inn. Pet-fee and restriction free for Fido, humans can take advantage of the complimentary evening kick back and breakfast the next morning before heading out for another fun-filled day of play together. Always a great choice, this Drury Inn is located at 2220 Northwood Boulevard.

WHERE TO SIT & STAY

COTTAGES ON STOUTS CREEK

The Cottages on Stouts Creek are located next to the Plain & Fancy B&B just a couple of miles east of Arcadia on Highway 72 and make for a welcome retreat after a busy day of exploring with Mother Nature. The cottages are cozy but spacious with room for six. With full kitchens, dining tables, open family rooms, and washers and dryers, it feels almost like home. Enjoy the semi-private back patios along Stouts Creek for relaxing evenings and morning coffee. Guests are welcome to use the pool at the Plain & Fancy B&B or fish in the creek. There are plenty of places to walk your furry friend, but for late-night potty breaks you may want to stick to the grassy areas in front of the cottages. For daylight strolls you'll want to venture down by the cottage and creek to admire the beauty of the land. Guests are limited to two pets, and a minimal charge for the first one is $15. A second pet increases the total fee to $20. Weekly fees run $75 for the first pet and $25 for the second.

COTTAGE AT THE LOW WATER BRIDGE

Affiliated with the Plain & Fancy B&B, guests have all the same amenities as those staying in one of the Cottages on Stouts Creek and more. Located on the other side of the creek on a 250-acre working cattle farm, this property has two bedrooms and two baths, an electric fireplace, sleeper sofa, and flat-screen TV. A large deck overlooks Stouts Creek, and the cottage even has a garage. Visit www.missouricottages.com for rates and availability.

JOHNSON'S SHUT-INS STATE PARK

Johnson's Shut-Ins is one of only a few Missouri state parks that now offers pet-friendly cabins, with accommodations for four to six. With a queen-size bed, futon, electricity, heat and AC, ceiling fan, compact fridge, and microwave, you and your pup will hardly be roughing it. While the cabins do not have running water, the restroom and shower house are within walking distance and open all year. Each cabin has both a pedestal grill and campfire grill along with a picnic table and porch bench out front. Campers do need to bring their own cooking and camping gear as well as linens and towels. For those wanting to spend a large amount of time within Johnson's Shut-Ins and prefer some modern conveniences, cabins 1, 5, and 6 allow guests to bring two dogs. The rate is $75 per night, and some minimums do apply. Visit www.mostateparks.com or call 877-422-6766 for detailed information and to make a reservation.

BEST BITES

BAYLEE JO'S BBQ SEAFOOD AND GRILL

With award-winning barbeque that is slow smoked over cherry wood, Baylee Jo's (named after the owner's daughter) is *the* place to go in Ironton. The covered outdoor area made of cedar and pine allows you and your pup to dine together almost any time of year, and the drive-thru is a convenient option for people traveling with their dogs. The menu offers just about any meal you could imagine at a BBQ joint and then some. There are lots of seafood choices, including Cajun crawfish and Alaskan king crab legs as well as steaks and pizza. Of course, Baylee Jo's offers all the popular barbeque sides, but they turn it up a notch. Be sure to try the jalapeño hushpuppies. Located at 1315 N. Highway 21, it's easy to see why it was voted "Editor's Choice" by the *St. Louis Post-Dispatch*.

RYNO'S PUB, PIZZERIA & GRILL

Just south of Ironton, in what seems like the middle of nowhere, Ryno's serves up St. Louis–style pizzas baked in a firebrick oven along with appetizers, salads, burgers, sandwiches, pasta, steaks, seafood, and even gumbo. You won't find a restaurant this good for miles, so kick back amidst the pines with Fido and enjoy the live music, some good food, and a cocktail. Find Ryno's Pub on Facebook or call 573-546-1234 for directions.

SOUTHEAST REGION

CAPE GIRARDEAU

Jean Baptiste de Girardot started a trading post on a rock jutting out into the Mississippi River in the 1730s. This piece of land that projected prominently out in the river was referred to as the "Cape," and while Girardot didn't stay long, his name remained associated with the area. Pride within Cape Girardeau is quite evident, with murals depicting significant figures of the past at every turn, stories of this river settlement galore, and too-many-to-count historical sites. Cape Girardeau honors its past, but also entertains visitors with many modern activities.

Fido Fact

Famous talk-radio host and author Rush Hudson Limbaugh III was born and raised in Cape Girardeau. Visitors can drive by numerous buildings important to his past, such as the radio station where he first started his broadcasting career as a teen and his childhood home. The controversial host is a dog lover and speaks often about Abbey and Welleslley, his Old English Sheepdogs.

PARKS & TRAILS FOR TAILS

CAPE ROCK PARK

Cape Rock Park is home to one of several scenic overlooks in the city and was Girardot's original trading post. Upon visiting this park—which encompasses over twenty-one acres of mostly preserved land—visitors find an unforgettable sight of the Mississippi River and picnic tables and benches where they can stay awhile to enjoy the view. This scenic overlook can be found off of Cape Rock Drive.

TRAIL OF TEARS STATE PARK

This park honors the many Cherokee Indians who lost their lives while crossing the Mississippi River in the 1830s under harsh winter weather conditions while relocating to Oklahoma. Today there are numerous trails for hikers, fishing sites off the Mississippi or the well-stocked Lake Boutin, and picnic and campsites, all of which make this park an outdoor haven for you and your pup. With some of the prettiest scenery in the state, lookouts provide stunning views, and visitors can watch bald eagles during the winter months near the cliffs and bluffs. For additional campground information and hours of the Visitor Center, go to www.mostateparks.com/trailoftears.htm.

RIVERWALK TRAIL

One of your first stops in Cape should be downtown by the riverfront. After many years of flood devastation to this area, a fifteen-foot floodwall was built in 1964. The floodwall has proven to be a savior to the livelihood of downtown Cape Girardeau. The 1,100-foot-long wall is not only functional, but an attraction in itself: the Mississippi River Tales Mural depicts the city's founding and history. Lewis & Clark, the Trail of Tears, and the Civil War are just a few of the features in this twenty-four-panel piece of art. After admiring the Mighty Mississippi and the mural, you and your pup will want to explore the mile-long trail along the river, and if you visit between the months of April and November you can indulge in some fresh produce or even arts and crafts at the farmers' market.

SIGHTS & EVENTS WORTH A LICK

BOLLINGER MILL STATE HISTORIC SITE GRISTMILL AND COVERED BRIDGE

A place of great natural beauty, this site provides the perfect place for a picnic with your pup and is quite popular with artists and professional photographers. Home to the oldest covered bridge remaining in Missouri and a nineteenth-century grain gristmill, Bollinger Mill State Historic Site is named for George Bollinger, who built the first gristmill on the property (the one standing now is the last of three built here) and brought twenty families from North Carolina to settle on these grounds. The bridge was built in 1858 by Joseph Lansmon and is open only to pedestrians today. The mill and bridge sit at 113 Bollinger Mill Road in Burfordville and are open daily from dawn to 10 p.m. with tours of the gristmill offered for a minimal fee. Dogs are welcome on the grounds and bridge, but they are not allowed on the mill tour.

CIVIL WAR DRIVING TOUR

Cape Girardeau was no exception to the bloody battles or casualties of the Civil War. The Battle of Cape Girardeau would mark the first of many battle sites in Cape and occurred in April of 1863. See the only remaining fort (Fort D) of the four built in town, view the Longview House, or visit the Confederate and Union memorials. To schedule a guided tour of Fort D or to obtain information on the self-guided Civil War Driving Tour, contact the Cape Girardeau Convention and Visitors Bureau at 573-335-1631.

THE GREAT MURALS TOUR

No other city within the Show Me State does murals like Cape Girardeau! Pick up a Visitors Guide and head out with your pup to see the floodwall mural, Welcome to Cape Mural, the Coca-Cola Mural, the Riverfest Mural, the River Heritage Mural, and the Heritage of Music Mural, among others. The town also has indoor murals, but dog access could be problematic. The flood wall mural is the most popular and depicts almost fifty Missourians and other prominent figures who were significant to the state, such as Mark Twain, Jesse James, Rush Limbaugh, and President Truman, to name a few. The tiled Southeast Missourian Murals, located at Broadway and Lorimier, took a total of twelve years to complete and were the first of their kind in the country. Dedicated to the city for its two hundredth anniversary, the Bicentennial Mural is forty by twenty-two feet and tells the story of Cape's founding. This mural is located at 405 Broadway.

OLD MISSISSIPPI RIVER BRIDGE SCENIC OVERLOOK

Built in 1928, the bridge that once served as the "Gateway to the Ozarks" and served as a passage between the states of Missouri and Illinois barely remains. A small piece of the old bridge has been restored, but the real attraction here is the view of the river, which is unlike any other in town. Visitors of the overlook can use the viewing scope as well as the River Campus Trail, which borders the river. The River Campus property once housed St. Vincent's Seminary and is now home to the largest American beech tree of Missouri. Take your dog for a walk and take in the history explained through interpretive signage provided trailside. You'll find these interesting pieces of Cape's history at the corner of Spanish and Morgan Oak streets. Listed on the National Register of Historic Places, the Glenn House is worth driving by and a short distance from here at 325 S. Spanish Street. David A. Glenn, a prominent citizen that helped develop the city of Cape, built the home for his daughter in 1883. Originally a farmhouse style, the home was later converted to Queen Anne style and today is completely restored while still maintaining many of its original features.

OLD VINCENT'S CHURCH

The English Gothic Revival architecture is not only spectacular, but also rare in America. Fido isn't allowed to worship here, but if you can sneak a peek inside, you'll be awe-stricken. The outside of Old Vincent's is as magnificent as the inside, so you won't be disappointed with a visit to the exterior grounds. The church was built in 1853, and the original pews and altar are still in place. In addition to tours and cultural events, a Sunday Mass is still held. This beauty is located at 131 S. Main Street near the river and across from the Red House Interpretive Center.

SITES TO SEE DRIVING TOUR

Serious sightseers should purchase the Sites to See Driving Tour CD, which provides visitors with information on thirty-three of the most significant points of interest in town, along with a detailed map. This package is a mere five dollars and is available at the Convention and Visitors Bureau, which can be found at 400 Broadway in Suite 100.

TUNES AT TWILIGHT

Take a chair and your pup down to the Common Pleas Courthouse Gazebo for an hour-long free performance. The Friday evening outdoor musical concerts begin in May and run for six weeks.

TWIN OAKS VINEYARD & WINERY

With a covered pavilion perfectly placed by the beer garden and a large patio overlooking the majestic hillside, Twin Oaks offers guests good drink, scenic views, and live music (April through October). Twin Oaks is a must-stop for visitors traveling with their four-legged friends. Enter the grape-stomp contest or just sit back with a glass of one of their many award-winning wines and enjoy the peaceful atmosphere or live entertainment. Twin Oaks Vineyard is located off Highway F in Farmington, Missouri.

STE. GENEVIEVE

Follow I-55 north from Cape Girardeau to Ste. Genevieve, which was the first European settlement in the state of Missouri and boasts eighteenth- and nineteenth-century French- and Creole-inspired architecture. Each August, Ste. Genevieve hosts Jour de Fete, the premier arts and crafts fair of the Midwest. Aside from craft booths, visitors can enjoy music, wine tasting, and festival food along with displays and exhibits from the French Colonial days. The Felix Valle State Historic Site consists of several buildings built in the early 1800s and is home to the French military camp reenactment as well as Colonial crafts demonstrations.

Reward your pup for his good behavior at the fair with a walk on one of the trails at Hawn State Park (just west of Ste. Genevieve off Route 32). One of the state's most unusual headwater streams (naturally carved through sandstone bedrock and a shut-ins stream) exists on the one-mile Pickle Creek Trail. For an extended hike, opt for the Whispering Pine Trail (considered one of the best in the state), which consists of both a four- and six-mile loop where hikers can view wildlife and unique landscapes.

Ste. Genevieve County is also home to Cave Vineyard, named for the saltpeter cave located on the property. Pack your own picnic lunch or get some cheese and sausage to nibble on while you and your furry friend take in the beauty of the vineyards and rolling hills from the pavilion where you are sure to encounter other canine friends. Cave Vineyard is located at 21124 Cave Road in Ste. Genevieve County.

WHERE TO SIT & STAY

DRURY SUITES

Among the most pet-friendly hotels are those by Drury. With renovations in 2012 and no pet fee or size limit, this is your best value in town. Not only does this hotel offer guests a free hot complimentary breakfast, but free hot food and cold beverages are also available in the evening. Two-room suites as well as extended-stay suites are available. This hotel is located at 3303 Campster Drive and will welcome both your pet and you. There is also a Drury Lodge in town, which is pet-friendly and located at 104 S. Vantage.

HAMPTON INN

Unlike many other Hampton Inns, this one is pet-friendly, welcomes dogs up to fifty pounds, and does not charge a pet fee. The hotel features a fitness center and offers a free hot breakfast, or a breakfast for the road for those who would rather eat on the run. The Hampton Inn is located at 103 Cape West Parkway.

BEST BITES

ANDY'S FROZEN CUSTARD

Take your furry friend to Andy's, where they'll offer up a scoop of the freshest ingredients just for him to lap up while you enjoy your own frozen treat. You can find Andy's Frozen Custard at 809 N. Kingshighway in Cape Girardeau among numerous other locations throughout Missouri and other Midwest states.

BEL AIR GRILL

Visit Bel Air at 24 S. Spanish Street for some good bar food on the large deck where you can catch a game on TV or enjoy live music with your furry friend. Be sure to order their specialty chips: the Bel Potatoes. The wings and steak sandwich are also good choices at this pet-friendly establishment.

BELLA ITALIA RISTORANTE

For the best Italian food in town and where they welcome your four-legged friend with a dish of water, head to the patio of Bella Italia at 20 N. Spanish. With the Mighty Mississippi flowing nearby, you can enjoy a filling dinner of Cape's finest pasta, steak, or seafood along with one of their many wine choices or a craft, import, or domestic beer. The only problem you'll have at this restaurant is choosing from their extensive menu of scrumptious Italian cuisine. Bella Italia is open for lunch and dinner and offers Happy Hour pricing.

SOUTHEAST REGION: CAPE GIRARDEAU

CUP 'N CORK

Located in Cape's historic downtown, this coffee house/café is the ideal choice for you and Fido to grab a gourmet coffee, a glass of wine, and some lunch or dinner on the front patio. This establishment offers guests a full menu of soups, salads, and sandwiches along with melt-in-your-mouth homemade desserts for humans. They invite man's best friend to enjoy a **doggie biscuit** along with a cool drink from the water bowl on the porch. Cup 'n Cork is located at 46 N. Main Street just off the Mississippi River.

RIVER RIDGE WINERY

River Ridge Winery, off County Road 321 in Commerce, welcomes supervised dogs that play well with others as their human companions enjoy a glass of wine with lunch or dinner. Cozy up to the fire pit on cooler days and enjoy peaceful settings or live music from the many patios and pavilions. The lunch menu is extensive, with everything from picnic baskets to appetizers, salads, sandwiches, and desserts. Specials like crab cakes with Maw Maw's slaw and their world-famous chili are available on the weekends.

POSH PUPPY

BUSCH PET PRODUCTS

With an extensive supply of products—many of which are locally and American made—along with high-quality holistic and all-natural foods, Busch Pet Products is worth a visit. They also offer a dog wash and spa along with seasonal events such as pictures for Valentine's Day, a summer luau, and their fall **Pet Fest,** to name a few. As a partner for local adoption agencies, they host numerous events throughout the year. For additional information and to view adorable pics of event participants, visit their website at buschpetproductscare.intuitwebsites.com.

MISSISSIPPI MUTTS

For a fetchin' good time go to Mississippi Mutts on Broadway where there's always something exciting going on and where you'll find products and services for all of your pup's needs and wants. Treat her to a spa day at the self-grooming station, pick up a unique new toy, and stock up on organic **fresh-baked treats.** There's a large selection of Cardinals' gear (essential for all canine fans) and lots of furry friends to sniff out. Mississippi Mutts is a dedicated supporter of the Humane Society and the hippest place in town for both you and your pooch to visit.

SLOAN + THEMIS

For vintage and upcycled jewelry, visit Sloan + Themis where original pieces are created with quality beads and other unique finds by owner/designer Claire Bruce. This small retailer welcomes your canine to shop with you and prides itself on being eco-friendly while supporting both local and global artisans that create with their hands as opposed to industrial machines. This shop is located at 31C N. Main Street in the historic area.

PLACES AND NAMES INDEX

Arcadia, 163
Arcadia Valley, 163-172
Bagnell Dam, 77, 80-81
Battle of Cape Girardeau, 176
Battle of Carthage, 13-15
Battle of Kirksville, 30
Battle of Pilot Knob, 166-167
Battle of Westport, 2
Starr, Belle, 143
Bingham, George Caleb, 39, 74
Boone, Daniel, 87
Boonville, 40-41
Branson, 127-138
"Breakthrough," 50, 52
Burden, Charles, 7
Busch Stadium, 106-108, 113-114
Butcher, Samuel J., 142, 145
Cape Girardeau, 173-184
Carthage, 139-146
Central West End, 97, 101, 116, 118, 121
Charles Lohman Building, 67
Chillicothe, 14-20
Churchill, Winston, 50, 52-53, 55
  Rufus, 53
Clark, William, 61, 71, 90-91, 93
Columbia, 35-46
Country Club Plaza, 1-2, 4-6, 9-11, 13
Daniel Boone (Missouri's First Dog), 72
Davis, Lowell, 143
Defiance, 123-125
Dog's Tail, A, 24
Drum, 7
Dufur, Brett, 58
Forest Park, 101-102, 106, 112, 116

Fort Davidson State Historic Site, 167
Fulton, 47-56
Fuqua, Chad, 128, 130
Gasconade County Historical Society, 60
Gateway Arch, 101, 107, 114
Grim, Randy, 109
Hannibal, 21-27
Hermann, 57-66
Hickok, Wild Bill, 147
Ironton, 163
Jefferson City, 67-76
Jesse James, 177
Jim the Wonder Dog, 13
Kansas City, 1-13
Kartsonakis, Dino, 137
Katy Trail, 35, 37, 41, 58, 62, 65, 68-69, 89-91, 125
Kirksville, 28-34
Kirkwood, 107
Knox, John, 153
Lake of the Ozarks, 77-86
Lewis, Meriwether, 61, 71, 90-91, 93
Limbaugh, Rush, 173, 177
Loop, The, 101, 108-109, 114
Macon, 32
Marshall, 13
Missouri State Capitol, 67-68, 70-73, 75-76
National World War I Museum, 3
Nixon, Georganne Wheeler, 72
Nixon, Governor Jay, 72
Osage Beach, 56, 80-81, 84-86
Osage River, 77, 80
Pilot Knob, 163

Poplar Bluff, 168-169
Rocheport, 35
St. Charles, 87-100
Ste. Genevieve, 179
St. Joseph, 18
St. Louis, 101-121
Sandys, Edwina, 52
Seaman, 71, 90, 93, 95
Soulard, 97, 101, 111, 116, 120
Springfield, 147-162
Stephens College, 42
Stray Rescue, 109, 118
Thatcher, Margaret, 55
Truman, Harry S., 28, 31, 177
Truman, Margaret, 28
Twain, Mark, 21-22, 24-25, 27, 177
Warrensburg, 7
Wentzville, 88, 104
Whine Trail, The, 122-126

ACCOMMODATIONS INDEX

Apfelbaum Cottage (Hermann), 62
Belle's Painted Lady (Hannibal), 26
Best Western Precious Moments Hotel (Carthage), 145
Big Cedar Lodge (Branson), 134
Boone's Colonial Inn (St. Charles), 95
Brashear House (Kirksville), 33
Camden on the Lake (Lake of the Ozarks), 82
Capitol Plaza Hotel (Jefferson City), 73
Casa De Loco (Lake of the Ozarks), 82
Chateau on the Lake Resort Spa & Convention Center (Branson), 135
Cheshire Inn (St. Louis), 112
Cottage at the Low Water Bridge (Arcadia Valley), 171
Cottage Grove Bed & Breakfast (Kirksville), 33
Cottages on Stouts Creek (Arcadia Valley), 170
Days Inn Chillicothe (Chillicothe), 19
Drury Inn (Columbia), 41
Drury Inn (Poplar Bluff), 169
Drury Inn (St. Charles), 95
Drury Inn (St. Louis), 112
Drury Suites (Cape Girardeau), 180
Econo Lodge Inn & Suites (Chillicothe), 19
Elms Hotel & Spa (Kansas City), 6
Four Seasons Hotel (St. Louis), 113
Hampton Inn (Cape Girardeau), 180
Hannibal Garden House (Hannibal), 26
Hermann Hill (Hermann), 63
Hilton Promenade at Branson Landing (Branson), 135
Hilton St. Louis at the Ballpark (St. Louis), 113
Holiday Inn Express (Fulton), 41
Homeaway.com (Branson), 136
Hotel Frederick (Boonville), 54
Innsbrook (St. Charles), 96
Johnson's Shut-Ins State Park (Arcadia Valley), 171
KOA Campground (Springfield), 156
La Quinta (Columbia), 42
Lodge of the Four Seasons (Lake of the Ozarks), 83
Loganberry Inn (Fulton), 55
Millennium Hotel (St. Louis), 114
Moonrise Hotel (St. Louis), 114
Parson's House B&B (Whine Trail), 125
Phillips Place B&B (Macon), 32
Professional Management Group, Inc. (Lake of the Ozarks), 83
St. Joseph Holiday Inn Riverfront Historic Hotel (St. Joseph), 18
Sheraton Suites Country Club Plaza (Kansas City), 6
Stoney Creek Inn (Columbia), 42
Stoney Creek Inn (St. Joseph), 18
Su Casa B&B (Kansas City), 8
Super 8 (Whine Trail), 125
Truman Hotel & Conference Center (Jefferson City), 74
University Plaza & Convention Center (Springfield), 155
Walnut Street Inn (Springfield), 157
Westin Kansas City at Crown Center (Kansas City), 8

PARKS INDEX

Bark Park (Lake of the Ozarks), 78
Blind Boone Park (Warrensburg), 7
Brashear Park (Kirksville), 29
Brommelsiek (St. Charles), 88
Cape Rock Park (Cape Girardeau), 174
Castlewood State Park (St. Louis), 102
Central Missouri Master Gardeners' Demonstration Gardens (Jefferson City), 68
Central Park (Carthage), 140
Chad A. Fuqua Memorial Park (Branson), 128
Cosmo Park (Columbia), 36
Crowder State Park (Chillicothe), 15
Cruse Dog Park (Springfield), 148
Dogwood Canyon Nature Park (Branson), 129
DuSable Dog Park (St. Charles), 89
Elephant Rocks State Park (Arcadia Valley), 164
Forest Park (St. Louis), 102
Frontier Park (St. Charles), 89
Fulton Dog Park (Fulton), 48
Garth Nature Area (Columbia), 36
Grindstone Nature Area (Columbia), 37
Ha Ha Tonka (Lake of the Ozarks), 78
Dempsey Dog Park (Hannibal), 22
Hawn State Park (Ste. Genevieve), 179
Hermann City Park (Hermann), 58
Hinkson Woods Conservation Area (Columbia), 37
Indian Hills Park (Columbia), 38
Jacob L. Loose Park (Kansas City), 2
Jefferson Barracks Park (St. Louis), 102
Johnson's Shut-Ins State Park (Arcadia Valley), 164
Katy Trail (Hermann), 58
Katy Trail (St. Charles), 91
Keener Springs (Williamsville), 168
Kellogg Lake (Carthage), 140

Lake of the Ozarks State Park (Lake of the Ozarks), 79
Little Dixie Lake Conservation Area (Fulton), 48
Long Branch State Park (Macon), 32
Mark Twain State Park (Hannibal), 22
Mingo National Wildlife Refuge (Poplar Bluff), 168
Missouri River Pedestrian and Bike Bridge (Jefferson City), 68
North Jefferson City Dog Park (Jefferson City), 69
Paw Park (St. Louis), 103
Penn Valley Park (Kansas City), 2
Pepper Dog Park (Branson), 131
Pershing State Park (Chillicothe), 15
Pickle Creek Trail (Ste. Genevieve), 179
Quail Ridge Dog Park (St. Louis), 104
Queeny Park (St. Louis), 104
Riverview Park (Hannibal), 22
Riverwalk Trail (Cape Girardeau), 175
Rock Bridge Memorial State Park (Columbia), 38
Sequiota Park (Springfield), 149
Simpson Park (Chillicothe), 15
Springfield Conservation Nature Center Trails (Springfield), 149
Stinson Creek Trail (Fulton), 48
Table Rock Lake (Branson), 127
Table Rock Lake State Park (Branson), 131
Taum Sauk Mountain State Park (Arcadia Valley), 165
Thousand Hills State Park (Kirksville), 29
Trail of Tears State Park (Cape Girardeau), 174
Twin Lakes Recreation Area (Columbia), 38
Veterans Park (Fulton), 49
Wallace Backer Park (Fulton), 49
Wayside Waifs Bark Park (Kansas City), 3

RESTAURANTS AND SHOPPING INDEX

Adam Puchta Winery (Hermann), 66
All About Dogs & Cats (Springfield), 162
All Pet Supplies & Equine Center (Springfield), 162
American Bounty Restaurant and Wine Bar (Whine Trail), 126
Andy's Frozen Custard (Lake of the Ozarks), 84
Andy's Frozen Custard (Cape Girardeau), 181
Arris' Pizza (Fulton), 56
Augusta Brewing Co. (Whine Trail), 126
Bambino's (Springfield), 158
Bar Louie (Kansas City), 9
Baylee Jo's BBQ Seafood & Grill (Arcadia Valley), 172
Bel Air Grill (Cape Girardeau), 181
Bella Italia Ristorante (Cape Girardeau), 181
Bevo Mill (St. Louis), 115
Blue Bull Bar & Grill (Springfield), 159
Boathouse, The (St. Louis), 116
Boji Stone Café (Chillicothe), 20
Braddens (St. Charles), 97
Brio Tuscan Grill (Kansas City), 9
Brooksider Bar & Grill (Kansas City), 10
Busch Pet Products (Cape Girardeau), 183
Café Via Roma (Jefferson City), 75
Canine Cookies N Cream Dog Bakery (St. Charles), 99
Capitol City Cork & Provisions (Jefferson City), 75
Cassano's Pizza and Subs (Hannibal), 27

Cave Vineyard (Ste. Genevieve), 179
Chandler Hill Vineyards (Whine Trail), 123
Coffee Ethic (Springfield), 159
Coffee Zone (Columbia), 43
Cree Mee Drive-In (Lake of the Ozarks), 84
Creek Side Bistro (Springfield), 160
Cup 'N Cork (Cape Girardeau), 182
Dave's Famous Barbeque (Branson), 137
Dino's 24 Karrot Cake Café (Branson), 137
Dog Days Bar & Grill (Lake of the Ozarks), 85
Doggie Style Bowtique (Kansas City), 12
Dog's World of Fun (Kansas City), 12
Espresso Laine at the Junction (Hermann), 64
Foster's Martini & Wine Bar (St. Joseph), 18
Four Muddy Paws (St. Louis), 119
Friendly Paws Pet Boutique (Lake of the Ozarks), 86
Galloway Ice Cream Shoppe (Springfield), 160
Gordon Biersch Brewery Restaurant (Kansas City), 10
Granfalloon Restaurant & Bar (Kansas City), 10
Groomingdale's Pet Boutique (Hannibal), 23
Hawg Fathers BBQ (Macon), 32
Hayden's Drive-In (Poplar Bluff), 169
Hermann Wurst Haus (Hermann), 64
Hermannhoff Winery (Hermann), 66

Hicks Hometown Drive-In (Chillicothe), 20
Indian Hills Winery (Poplar Bluff), 168
Jake's on Main (St. Charles), 99
Java Jive Coffee House (Hannibal), 27
Jillsies (Hermann), 65
Kennelwood (St. Louis), 120
Labinnah Bistro (Hannibal), 27
La Dolce Vita Winery (Whine Trail), 123
Land of Paws (Kansas City), 12
Li'l Rizzos (Lake of the Ozarks), 85
Lizzi & Rocco's Natural Pet Market (Columbia), 46
Llywelyn's Pub (St. Charles), 97
Llywelyn's Pub (St. Louis), 116
Lola & Penelope's Premiere Pet Boutique (St. Louis), 119
Madison's Café (Jefferson City), 76
Mike & Zach's BBQ To-Go (Poplar Bluff), 169
Milano's Italian Restaurant (Kirksville), 34
Mixx, The (Kansas City), 11
Mississippi Mutts (Cape Girardeau), 184
Mount Pleasant Estates (Whine Trail), 123
Old Millstream Inn Restaurant and Beer Garden (St. Charles), 98
Pets in the CIty (St. Louis), 120
Picasso's Coffee House (St. Charles), 98
Pi Pizzeria (St. Louis), 115
Red Mango (Columbia), 43
Ricky's Chocolate Box (Hermann), 65
River Ridge Winery (Cape Girardeau), 182
Rue Lafayette Café (St. Louis), 117
R.T. Weiler's Food and Spirits (St. Charles), 87
Rymac's Rub N Pub (Springfield), 161

Ryno's Pub, Pizzeria & Grill (Arcadia Valley), 172
Saults Drug Store (Fulton), 47
Shakespeare's Pizza (Columbia), 44
Shiloh Bar & Grill (Columbia), 44
Sloan + Themis (Cape Girardeau), 184
Sparky's Homemade Ice Cream (Columbia), 44
Square One Brewery & Distillery (St. Louis), 117
SqWires Restaurant (St. Louis), 118
Steve's Garden Deli (Kirksville), 34
Stone HIll Winery (Hermann), 66
Ted Drewes Frozen Custard (St. Louis), 118
Texas Land & Cattle Steak House (Branson), 138
Three Dog Bakery (Kansas City), 13
Trailside Bar & Grill (Hermann), 65
Trailside Cafe & Bike Shop (Columbia), 35
Treats Unleashed (St. Charles), 100
Treats Unleashed (St. Louis), 121
True Vision One (St. Louis), 121
Upper Crust Bakery (Columbia), 45
Vine Wine Bar & Bistro (St. Charles), 98
Vintage Paris Coffee & Wine Café (Branson), 138
Whisler's Hamburgers (Carthage), 146
Wild Flower (St. Louis), 118
Wine Cellar & Bistro (Columbia), 45
Wine Country Gardens (Whine Trail), 124
Wing Shack Grill & Bar (Springfield), 160
Winslow's BBQ (Kansas City), 11
Wolfgang's Pet Shop (St. Louis), 121
Yanis Coffee Zone (Jefferson City), 76
Yellow Farmhouse Vineyard (Whine Trail), 124
Yuppy Puppy Pet Spa (St. Charles), 100
Zesto (Jefferson City), 76

SIGHTS AND EVENTS INDEX

66 Drive-In Theatre (Carthage), 144
American Kennel Club Museum of the Dog (St. Louis), 105
APA's Canine Carnival (St. Louis), 106
Arrow Rock (Columbia), 39
Art in the Park (Columbia), 39
Autumn Historic Folklife Festival (Hannibal), 23
Bacon Fest (Kirksville), 30
Bagnell Dam Strip and Overlook (Lake of the Ozarks), 80
BarBQ & Brats Festival (Hermann), 59
Bark in the Park (Kansas City), 4
Bark in the Park (St. Louis), 106
Bark in the Park (Springfield), 150
Bark in the Park at Hammons Field (Springfield), 150
Battle of Carthage State Historic Site (Carthage), 141
Battle of Kirksville (Kirksville), 30
Berlin Wall and "Breakthrough" (Fulton), 52
Bollinger Mill State Historic Site Gristmill and Covered Bridge (Cape Girardeau), 176
Branson Ghost & Legends Walking Tour (Branson), 132
Branson Landing Fountains (Branson), 132
Buster's Old Time Photos (Branson), 133
Canine Cannonball (Lake of the Ozarks), 80
Capital Jazzfest (Jefferson City), 70
Chautauqua in the Park (Chillicothe), 16

Chillicothe Downtown Walking Tour (Chillicothe), 17
Christmas Traditions (St. Charles), 92
Church of St. Mary the Virgin, Aldermanbury (Fulton), 52
Cider Days (Springfield), 151
City Garden (St. Louis), 106
Civil War Driving Tour (Arcadia Valley), 167
Civil War Driving Tour (Cape Girardeau), 176
Disc Dogs (St. Louis), 107
Dog Days Celebration (St. Louis), 107
Dog Daze of Summer (Chillicothe), 16
Dog Fest (Springfield), 151
Dog Retreat at the Elms (Kansas City), 5
Dog Swim (Springfield), 152
Dog Swim–Kirkwood (St. Louis), 107
Downtown Audio/Video Walking Tour (Jefferson City), 70
Fall Color Driving Tour (Poplar Bluff), 168
Fantastic Caverns (Springfield), 152
Felix Valle State Historic Site (Ste. Genevieve), 179
Fete de Glace (St. Charles), 92
Fort Davidson State Historic Site (Arcadia Valley), 166
Gateway Arch (St. Louis), 107
General Ulysses S. Grant Statue (Arcadia Valley), 167
Governor's Mansion (Jefferson City), 72
Great Murals Tour (Cape Girardeau), 177
Hermann City Cemetery Walk

(Hermann), 60
Hermann Walking Tours (Hermann), 61
Hermann Wurstfest (Hermann), 59
"Hit the Crik" Crawdad Eating Contest (Fulton), 56
Iron County Court House (Arcadia Valley), 167
Jacob's Vineyard & Winery (Kirksville), 30
Jour de Fete (Ste. Genevieve), 179
Kansas City Walking Tours (Kansas City), 5
Kendrick Place (Carthage), 141
Laumeier Sculpture Park (St. Louis), 108
Lewis and Clark Boat House and Nature Center (St. Charles), 93
Lewis and Clark Trailhead Plaza (Jefferson City), 71
Living Windows Festival (Columbia), 39
Locust Creek Covered Bridge (Chillicothe), 17
Loop Ice Carnival (St. Louis), 108
Lover's Leap (Hannibal), 25
Maastricht Friendship Tower (Warrensburg), 7
Maifest (Hermann), 60
Maple Leaf Festival (Carthage), 142
Mark Twain Boyhood Home (Hannibal), 25
Music on Main (St. Charles), 93
National Churchill Museum (Fulton), 50
National Tom Sawyer Days (Hannibal), 25
Nelson-Atkins Museum of Art (Kansas City), 4
Oktoberfest (Hermann), 60
Oktoberfest (St. Charles), 93
Old Mississippi River Bridge Scenic Overlook (Cape Girardeau), 177
Old Vincent's Church (Cape Girardeau), 178
Oma & Noma Heritage Festival (Lake of the Ozarks), 81
Oovvda Winery (Springfield), 152
Paws in the Park (Columbia), 40
Pets & Pumpkins (Springfield), 154
Pooch Promenade (Macon), 32
Pooches in the Ballpark (St. Louis), 108
Precious Moments Chapel & Gardens (Carthage), 142
Prehistoric Native American Burial Mounds (Columbia), 40
Purina Farms (St. Louis), 110
Red Barn Arts & Crafts Festival (Kirksville), 31
Red Oak II (Carthage), 143
St. Louis Walk of Fame (St. Louis), 109
Serenity Valley Winery (Fulton), 51
Seven Springs Winery (Lake of the Ozarks), 81
Soulard Mardi Gras (St. Louis), 111
Sites to See Driving Tour (Cape Girardeau), 178
State Capitol (Jefferson City), 72
Strut Your Mutt (St. Louis), 110
Taste of St. Louis (St. Louis), 111
Trails for Tails (St. Charles), 94
Truman State University (Kirksville), 31
Tunes at Twilight (Cape Girardeau), 178
Twin Oaks Vineyard & Winery (Cape Girardeau), 178
Twin Spires Cathedral (St. Joseph), 18
Veterans Memorial (Kirksville), 31
Veterans Memorial (St. Charles), 94
Victorian Home Driving Tour (Carthage), 144
Walking History Tour of Boonville (Columbia), 40
Wilson's Creek National Battlefield (Springfield), 154
Woofstock (Kansas City), 5